NEWPORT BAY *A Pioneer History*

By *ELLEN K. LEE*

NEWPORT BAY

A Pioneer History

Foreword by DON C. MEADOWS

Newport Beach Historical Society

Sultana Press: Fullerton   1973

Foreword

USUALLY, local histories are of two kinds: nostalgic accounts drawn from faulty memories or cold academic dissertations that provide facts but little human interest. In *Newport Bay*, Ellen Lee has written a happy combination of personal knowledge and a rare gift of research. From association she finds warmth and color in an area that was her home, and from research she answers many old questions that have baffled historians. She also solves the mystery of *Quigara*. She has seined rays of historical enlightenment from the bay and has held a Tournament of Lights on a steady course through the tide lands that became a sparkling city. Many points are in the offing, so sail on, for broad sweeps of knowledge lie ahead.

DON C. MEADOWS

Santa Ana, California
September 26, 1973

Acknowledgments

FOR photographs and source materials the writer is indebted to Orange County historians Don C. Meadows and Jim Sleeper, and to Miss Elizabeth Karshner and Mr. Roger B. Berry of Special Collections of the Library at the University of California, Irvine; Miss Linda Herman and the staff of Special Collections of the Library at California State University, Fullerton; Miss Mary Wilkins, Anaheim Public Library; Mrs. Sylvia Arden, Serra Museum, San Diego; Mrs. Margaret Key, Bowers Museum, Santa Ana; Mr. James E. Ballinger of the Orange County Harbors, Beaches, and Parks District; Bancroft Library, University of California, Berkeley; Los Angeles County Museum; Mrs. Barbara Conn, the Irvine Company; Mariners Museum, Newport News, Virginia; U.S. Coast and Geodetic Survey; California State Library, Sacramento; Los Angeles Public Library; California Room of the San Diego Public Library; and the Reference Department of the Santa Ana Public Library.

Individuals who have generously aided in this project over a period of several years are Mr. Arthur J. McFadden, Mrs. William B. Worden, Mrs. George H. Rasmussen, Mr. Harold T. Brewer, Mr. Rufus B. Courtney, Mr. George G. Key, Mrs. Stanley Le Lievre, Mrs. W. B. Lockett, Mr. Ivan L. Peterson, Mr. E. H. Salter, Mrs. Donald S. Smiley, Mr. and Mrs. Howard L. Smith, Miss Louise Tubbs, Mrs. Philip J. Burton, the late Mrs. Grace Crosier, Mr. M. L. de Grasse, Mrs. Mary Dickson, the late Mrs. Agnes McMillan Ellsworth, Mr. Joseph M. Ferguson, Mr. and Mrs. Roland G. Ghriest, Mrs. Everett G. Hager, Mrs. Ella Hemstreet, the late Miss Lillian Lindenberger, Mr. Ralph P. Maskey, Mrs. C. W. Messing, the late Mrs. Josephine Oquist, Mr. Paul A. Palmer, Mr. Richard L. Patterson, Mr. George W. Peabody, Miss Edna Phelps, Mr. John A. Siegel, Mrs. W. Donald Smith, and Mrs. Harry Welch.

For reading the manuscript and making helpful suggestions concerning its revision the writer is indebted to Dr. Henry Cord Meyer, Professor of History at U.C. Irvine. From the beginning of this project Mrs. Dorothea M. Sheely, Newport Beach city librarian, has been a source of constant support and encouragement. Mrs. Felicia M. Young of the Corona del Mar branch of the Newport Beach Public Library assisted in the selection of photographs from the collection of the Newport Beach Historical Society. Mr. Walter Mc Graw of the Mariners branch helped in making available the early editions of the Newport *News*. Miss Florence Crosier of Laguna Hills loaned the writer a collection of historic newspaper clippings saved by her mother, one of the founders of the Newport Beach Public Library.

Table of Contents

List of Illustrations

NEWPORT BAY *A Pioneer History*

An Uncharted Estuary /1

ON A WINDY September day in the year 1860, the United States Coast Survey schooner *Humboldt* dropped anchor in Pacific Ocean waters off a lonely beach known today as the Newport-Balboa peninsula. The silence of the place was broken only by the pounding surf and the cries of thousands of shore birds. Inside the barrier beach lay a marshy lagoon stretching five miles from west to east, the estuary through which the Santa Ana River flowed to the sea. Northward, at right angles to the lagoon, the upper bay extended inland for three and a half miles, surrounded by its picturesque high cliffs. In Spanish mission times this natural landlocked harbor was called *Bolsa de Gengara*; under Mexican rule it became *Bolsa de San Joaquin*. The first American settlers called it San Joaquin Bay, or San Joaquin Slough. Today the lagoon is Newport Harbor.

Aboard the *Humboldt*, Coast Survey Assistant William E. Greenwell prepared to disembark and make a preliminary survey of the uncharted shoreline and lagoon. Above them, as they looked inland, the survey party would have seen the seaward boundaries of two great cattle ranches, *Rancho Santiago de Santa Ana* and *Rancho San Joaquin*. They saw no human habitation on the mesa to the west or on the San Joaquin Hills to the east. Because of his courage and skill at taking small boats ashore through the surf, Captain Greenwell, 37, was known as the "best surfer" in the U.S. Coast Survey service.[1] He and his men lowered their boat and rowed into the entrance, located then about a half-mile down the peninsula from today's Balboa Pavilion. Like countless others in the years that followed, they discovered that the ever-shifting narrow inlet with its treacherous ground swells was a deadly trap. Greenwell "nearly lost his boat and crew."[2]

In a report to the Coast Survey, Greenwell noted that the five-mile-long lagoon was "separated from the ocean by a narrow strip of sand-beach, over which heavy southeast and northwest swells wash in every gale." Of the sandbar in the entrance he wrote, "Over this bar there is a frightful swell rolling and tumbling at all stages of the tide, making it dangerous to cross in boats of any kind."[3] Greenwell postponed further inspection until the following spring, but because of the Civil War he was recalled to the east coast. Fifteen years went by before the first hydrographic survey of Newport Bay was made. By that time the entrance had shifted eastward along the peninsula, closer to its present location at Corona del Mar. A small sternwheel steamer, the *Vaquero*, had entered in 1870 to establish a shipping business at Newport Landing, at the southwest end of the upper bay. From 1875 until 1889 the McFadden brothers' steamer *Newport* made regular voyages to and from northern California ports, entering the bay only at high tide and making her way cautiously through the shallow channel. When the McFaddens failed to obtain federal funds for harbor improvements, they abandoned their shipping port inside the bay and built a large ocean wharf at the site of the present-day Newport Beach municipal pier.

It was not until the twentieth century that the Santa Ana River was diverted from the lower bay, deep channels and turning basins dredged, marshlands filled, and the entrance stabilized by twin jetties. The first "harbor boosters" had envisioned a flourishing commercial harbor with industrial plants, railroad connections, and huge wharves at which the world's mightiest vessels could unload their cargoes. But a happier fate was in store for the former river lagoon. With the completion of the last reclamation projects in the spring of 1936, Newport Bay began its rise to fame as California's first and finest yachting and recreational harbor.

Today Newport Harbor is the home port of thousands of boats, its blue waters dotted with seven residential islands of unusual beauty. The city of Newport Beach, which began in 1889 as a wharfside community on the Newport-Balboa peninsula, has grown from its water-oriented areas onto the inland hills and mesa. Once sailors scanned the horizon to sight the peaks of *Old Saddleback*, the landmark guiding them to the entrance of Newport Bay. Today the tall buildings of Newport Center, visible on land and sea for many miles, stand as beacons of a modern city on what was once cattle ranch land above a lonely estuary.

Newport Landing

Bay entrance

Old Saddleback

"Newport Bay. A good landmark for making the bay is to bring the double-peaked Santiago Mountain . . . to bear northeast when the entrance to the bay is directly under it." *Pacific Coast Pilot*, 1889.

Bolsa de Gengara /2

N O ONE KNOWS what the contours of Newport Bay were during the thousands of years before its first accurate mapping by the U.S. Coast Survey in 1875. Geologists tell us that in the Pleistocene epoch a mighty ancestor of the Santa Ana River carved the deep canyon that is now the upper bay, and the submarine canyon offshore of the Newport Beach municipal pier. For a long time the upper bay was an estuary open to the Pacific. Beginning at the end of the Pleistocene, about ten or twelve thousand years ago, marine and estuarine deposits began to fill the once-deep canyon. Eventually sandbars were formed, platforms upon which marshlands later developed.

The Santa Ana River, throughout its history, has frequently overflowed its banks and changed its main channel. After flowing through the upper bay for thousands of years, perhaps intermittently, the river carved itself a westerly course across the featureless Downey Plain to Alamitos Bay. By the beginning of the Spanish mission period in the 1770s, the Santa Ana River was established in a channel across a broad flood plain between the Newport and Huntington Beach mesas.[1] It continued to break into its old Alamitos Bay channel in times of heavy flood, but has never re-established a channel through upper Newport Bay in historic times. Offshore of the flood plain

between the Newport and Huntington Beach mesas an offshore barrier beach formed, growing down the coast until it enclosed the lagoon that is now lower Newport Bay. The river, imprisoned behind the barrier beach, or sandspit, turned downcoast to flow through the lagoon and out to sea.

Authorities disagree as to the approximate date at which the sandspit (today's Newport-Balboa peninsula) completed its growth and reached almost to the rocky point at Corona del Mar. H. L. Sherman theorized in his *History of Newport Beach* (1931) that the sandspit grew all the way from the Huntington Beach mesa to a place opposite the east end of Lido Isle in a period of about thirty-three years, from 1825 to 1858. Sherman believed that the sandspit made its final spurt of growth, from the end of Lido Isle almost to Corona del Mar, in the single flood season of 1861-62. Sherman's theories are open to question in the light of U.S. Coast Survey findings in 1860 and existing records of the Mexican rancho period. As previously noted, Captain William Greenwell found the lagoon to be five miles long (the approximate present length of the lower bay) in 1860, more than a year before the floods of 1861-62 to which Sherman attributes the peninsula's last great spurt of growth.[2]

Early Mexican maps and documents show that the Santa

3

Ana River flowed in approximately its present channel at the beginning of Spanish mission times. The diseño, or map, of *Rancho Santiago de Santa Ana*, granted in 1810 to José Antonio Yorba and Juan Pablo Peralta, shows the *Bolsa de Gengara* at the seaward tip of the Newport mesa. It seems likely that the lower bay was in existence by the beginning of Spanish mission times, if not long before that. Perhaps the Indians had legends or traditions about the origins of Newport Bay, but they left only the mute evidence of ancient village sites.

Southern California Indians were first observed in the sixteenth century by Juan Rodríguez Cabrillo and his men who sailed up the coast in the caravels *San Salvador* and *Victoria*, claiming the land for the king of Spain. Cabrillo made no reference to any place that can be identified as Newport Bay, but on October 7, 1542 he anchored at Catalina Island. Natives invited the explorers ashore, "and put their bows and arrows on the ground. Launching into the water a fine canoe containing eight or ten Indians, they came out to the ships."[3] On the following day the Spaniards "came to the mainland in a large bay, which they named the Baia de Los Fumos on account of the many smokes they saw there." Historians believe the *Baia de Los Fumos* was either San Pedro Bay or Santa Monica Bay, and that the "smokes" were Indian fires. Other explorers passed by during the next two hundred years. Some drew rough maps of the California coastline, but none left any record of the Newport Bay area.

Spanish colonization of California began in 1769 with the overland journey of Don Gaspar de Portolá and his leather-jacket soldiers who crossed the future Orange County about ten miles inland from Newport Bay. They found the local Indians gentle and friendly, and gave Spanish names to Santiago Creek and the Santa Ana River. The establishment of two missions, San Gabriel in 1771 and San Juan Capistrano in 1776, resulted in the gradual disappearance of nearby Indian villages. Indians who went to San Gabriel were henceforth known as *Gabrielinos*; those in the vicinity of San Juan Capistrano were called *Juaneños*. Few names of the original Indian villages have survived but archives of Rancho Santiago de Santa Ana identify the Newport mesa as the location of *Genga*, or *Geng-Na*. Newport Bay was called *Bolsa de Gengara*, a name derived from the Indian name of the village. A. L. Kroeber's map of Southern California Indian rancherías shows a place called *Moyo* near Newport Center, but this name does not appear in the baptismal records of either mission and may refer to a landmark of some kind.

Although Genga and Moyo are the only Newport Bay place names still known today, the area contains many Indian sites. Some are believed to be only two centuries old; others existed thousands of years ago. Carbon dating of the skull of *Laguna woman*, found a number of years ago in Laguna Beach, indicates that there was human habitation along the Orange County coastline from 15,000 to 18,000 years ago.[4] Artifacts, skeletons, and midden (refuse) heaps of broken seashells and fire-blackened earth have been found along the banks of the Santa Ana River, at various locations on the Newport mesa, all around the upper bay, on headlands overlooking the ocean and lower bay, in the San Joaquin Hills, and in Big Canyon. An early observer, Nels C. Nelson, noted in 1912 that the new streets of Corona del Mar had been graded through an extensive old Indian campground. In 1964, before ground was broken for Newport Center, members of the Pacific Coast Archaeological Society unearthed several ancient Indian sites that are now covered by tall buildings. Indian relics found in the Newport Bay area include stone *manos* and *metates*, shell beads and fishhooks, obsidian arrow points, scrapers, and the beautifully worked "cogged stones," believed to have had a ceremonial significance.

California's coastal Indians lived in dome-shaped brush or tule huts, erected over frameworks of poles. Because of an abundance of food on land and shore, they were probably more permanent in their occupation of village sites than were the migratory inland peoples. Although Catalina Island and Santa Barbara Indians are known to have built large canoes of pine planks laced together, the boats most often used were *balsas*. These were rafts or canoes made of bundles of tules, tied into points at the ends and caulked with asphalt picked up along the beaches. Father Junípero Serra, founder of the California missions, wrote that he had seen Indians fishing from these frail craft, "with which they go a great way to sea." The question of whether Newport Bay Indians paddled tule rafts or the more intricately built plank canoes remains unanswered, but it seems likely

that they were familiar with both. Mainland Indians carried on an extensive trade with the Indians of Catalina Island, who brought heatproof steatite (soapstone) for implements and utensils.

Baptismal records of San Juan Capistrano Mission show that many residents of Genga became neophytes in the late 1770s and early 1780s. The first recorded baptism of an Indian from "ranchería de Genga" took place on May 24, 1778, when a fifteen year-old youth named *Lchainoque* received the Christian name of Alejandro.[5]

In 1810 Genga became a part of the 62,512 acre Rancho Santiago de Santa Ana, granted to the Yorbas and Peraltas. Stretching from the mountains to the sea this Spanish land grant included the modern cities of Santa Ana, Orange, Villa Park, Costa Mesa, and parts of Tustin and Newport Beach. Within the boundaries of the Yorba and Peralta grant the San Juan Capistrano friars continued to occupy a ranch on the mesa called the *estancia de Santa Ana*. Headquarters of the estancia were on the banks of the Santa Ana River, adjacent to the old Indian site. It is believed that the original adobe walls of the rebuilt Diego Sepúlveda Adobe in Costa Mesa may have been a part of the estancia headquarters.

In 1822, when Mexico won its independence from Spain, financial assistance for the missions was cut off. There had been other troubles for the Franciscans at San Juan Capistrano. Their great stone church, "Jewel of the Missions," built by Indian labor, had toppled in the 1812 earthquake. Many neophytes had died, victims of changes in their mode of living and of white men's diseases brought by Spanish soldiers. Floods in 1824-25 destroyed fields and vineyards; in the droughts that followed the padres turned to their estancia above the Santa

5

Ana flood plain.[6] While herds of cattle and sheep found water and pasturage in the river lowlands, the friars supervised the raising and storing of grain on the mesa. Several miles away, north of the upper bay, the mission had another outpost at a place called *San Joaquin*. San Joaquin overlooked the *Ciénega de Las Ranas* (Swamp of the Frogs), a then-undrained expanse of meadows and grasslands between the upper bay and present-day Tustin.

Although the Franciscans maintained these outposts in the Newport Bay area, and at one time suggested to the Mexican governor that he might consider ordering Mission San Juan Capistrano moved to the banks of the Santa Ana River, there is no evidence that they ever used the bay as a seaport. Their *embarcadero* was the cove south of San Juan Point, known today as Dana Point. Until Mexico became independent of Spain, only Spanish supply vessels anchored legally off San Juan Point, but others came. Among them was the frigate *Alexander*, given water and supplies by the friars in 1803. Six years later Aleut Indians lowered 24 canoes from Captain George W. Eayrs' *Mercury* and gathered 2117 otter skins before being ordered to leave.[7] In 1818 Argentine revolutionary Hippolyte Bouchard and his men sailed in on the *Santa Rosa* and *Argentina*, pillaged the "king of Spain's" stores at San Juan Capistrano, drank quantities of the padres' fine wine, and departed. Such bold ventures gave way in Mexican times after 1822 to a businesslike trade with American ships that sailed around the Horn from New England for cargoes of hides and tallow obtained from the long-horned Spanish cattle. Richard Henry Dana, a youth of nineteen when he left Boston in 1835 as a sailor aboard the brig *Pilgrim*, has described the trade at San Juan Capistrano in his great sea narrative, *Two Years Before the Mast*. The *Pilgrim* anchored a considerable distance offshore, sailors rowed in through the surf, and hides were thrown to the beach from the towering cliff above.

The decline of the missions had already begun at the time of Dana's visit to California. In 1834 the Mexican government issued a secularization order which, combined with insistent demands for land from an increasing number of *paisanos*, brought an end to the mission system in California. The Franciscans were powerless against encroachments upon their vast holdings. Mexican governors began making generous grants of land to their friends. Sent to face life in an outside world for which they were unprepared, mission Indians drifted to ranchos, towns, and inland mountain areas. Many became homeless wanderers. In a few decades their race was nearly extinct. The estancia at the old Genga Indian site reverted to the owners of Rancho Santiago de Santa Ana. In 1837 José Sepúlveda asked Governor Juan B. Alvarado for a grant of San Joaquin and the pasturelands of Ciénega de Las Ranas. The Newport Bay area was about to have a new owner.

Diseño of Rancho San Joaquin, as presented to the United States Land Commission in 1853, showing holdings that stretched along the coast from today's Irvine Avenue to Laguna Beach. Upper Newport Bay, at the left, is shown as open to the sea. A lower bay existed in Sepúlveda's day, but offshore sandspits and marshlands were of little interest to Mexican *rancheros.*

Don José Sepúlveda /3

IN 1837 JOSÉ ANDRÉS SEPÚLVEDA, 35, a citizen of the small pueblo of Los Angeles, received a grant of Rancho Ciénega de Las Ranas, a swampy inland area stretching from today's Orange County airport toward El Toro. Sepúlveda's cattle soon strayed in all directions across the boundaries of his grant. Yorbas, Peraltas, and the San Juan Capistrano fathers complained that Sepúlveda's holdings had not been measured according to Mexican law. The padres further accused the newcomer of stealing their cattle from the *ciénega*, while extending his holdings "to whereon and in a manner he pleased." His answer was an appeal to the governor for the additional lands he occupied, including the San Joaquin Hills and Newport Bay. Sepúlveda called the bay *Bolsa de San Joaquin*, although records show that the Yorbas and Peraltas still referred to it as *Bolsa de Gengara*.

Prefect Santiago de Argüello, investigating the matter for Governor Alvarado, reported that Sepúlveda "was a slippery and dishonest person who persistently and willfully sought to mislead the lawful authorities . . . that the diseño (map) accompanying the petition was drawn on such a distorted scale as to make the ranch appear about a tenth as large as it really was," and that he had "deliberately extended his boundaries from the beach on the south to the mountains on the north." On May 13, 1842, however, the governor granted Sepúlveda's request for his original Rancho Ciénega de Las Ranas, and an extension including *Bolsa de San Joaquin*. Henceforth the two grants would be known as Rancho San Joaquin.

Three weeks later, on June 4, 1842, Sepúlveda set off on horseback for a hill at the north end of Laguna Beach. Accompanying him were Manuel Domínguez, Justice of the Peace from Los Angeles, two witnesses named Antonio Coronel and Joaquin de Los Rios y Ruiz, and two cord bearers. A cord of braided rawhide fifty varas (about 137½ feet) in length was examined and approved by Domínguez, who ordered wooden stakes tied to the ends. One of the stakes was set in the ground and the other handed to a cord bearer, who galloped off with it up the canyon. When the cord was taut, the second stake was placed in the ground and the first pulled up to be carried beyond it to the next stopping place. In this manner the men measured a tract stretching north to the Santa Ana Mountains, west to Red Hill, south to the mainland shore of Newport Bay at a point above the middle of today's Lido Isle, and back along the seacoast to the point of beginning. An official document

Don Bernardo Yorba was one of the owners of Rancho Santiago de Santa Ana, which included land bordering the western end of the lower bay.

recording the measurement of the boundaries was signed by all except the cord bearers, who did not know how to read or write.[1]

The granting of Rancho San Joaquin, a tract of more than 47,000 acres, was an important event in the history of the Newport Bay region. For the first time, a single individual owned all the land around the upper bay and most of the inland shore of the lower bay, from Corona del Mar to the bluffs at the end of today's Irvine Avenue. Thirty-four years later, in 1876, the first James Irvine became sole owner of this grant and of an adjoining parcel of Rancho Santiago de Santa Ana that gave him most of the rest of the Newport Bay mainland shoreline. Irvine instituted the policy, followed by his son, the second James Irvine, and by the Irvine Company, of holding lands for agriculture and other purposes instead of subdividing and selling as soon as potential buyers appeared. This policy has greatly influenced the development of Orange County and the Newport Harbor area.

Sepúlveda repaired the mission's first structure on the San Joaquin Ranch and "built a better one, of adobe." A few years later he bought another house, *El Refugio*, within the boundaries of the neighboring Santiago de Santa Ana grant. This became his ranch headquarters where he lived with all the splendor of the typical *ranchero* of the "days of the dons." Sepúlveda and his wife, Francisca Ávila, parents of fourteen children, also had an adobe town house in Los Angeles.

In 1848 Mexican rule gave way to American occupation of California. The Gold Rush began in 1849, ushering in a period of undreamed-of prosperity for the great landowners of Southern California. Previously the long-horned cattle had been mainly a source of hides and tallow. Now, as thousands of meat-hungry men camped in the northern gold fields, the *rancheros* sent cattle north "on the hoof" and spent the abundant proceeds on bigger adobe houses and everything the Yankee ships could bring to fill them. Sepúlveda spent lavishly for elaborate clothing, fine horses, gambling, and entertaining. His fiestas, rodeos, and generous hospitality drew guests from all over Southern California.

Sepúlveda is said to have owned 3000 horses and 14,000 cattle. Legend has it that mares were separated into mañadas, according to the color of their coats, and that Sepúlveda liked to sit on his veranda and have them paraded before him. A superb horseman, he posed in 1856 for the famous equestrian portrait by Henri Penelon that hangs in Bowers Museum in Santa Ana. There was probably nothing Sepúlveda enjoyed more than horse races held on dusty roads near Los Angeles. In 1851 he bought an Australian mare, "Black Swan," to race against a gray stallion, "Sarco," owned by Pio Pico and Teodosio Yorba. All Southern California turned out to watch the event. Wagers were enormous. Francisca, Sepúlveda's wife, arrived on the scene with a handkerchief filled with gold slugs so that she and her friends might bet on Black Swan. When the mare won the race, Sepúlveda collected "twenty-five thousand dollars in cash, five hundred horses, five hundred mares, five hundred heifers, five hundred calves, and five hundred sheep."[2]

While José Sepúlveda divided his time between rancho and pueblo, the many owners of Rancho Santiago de Santa Ana, bordering the western end of Newport Bay, became leading pioneer agriculturists. Although several adobe houses stood near the old estancia site by the 1850s, most of the Yorbas and Peraltas and their relatives prefer-

Don José Sepúlveda

In 1842 Don José Sepúlveda became the first individual to own all the land around the upper bay and most of the mainland shoreline of the lower bay.

red to live farther inland. Tomás Yorba, one of the four sons of Jose Antonio Yorba, lived at a settlement known as Santa Ana (now Olive), northeast of today's city of that name. Here he maintained a store in addition to his ranch establishment. Alfred Robinson, agent for Bryant, Sturgis, and Co., hide shippers, described Tomás Yorba as "a tall, lean personage, dressed in all the extravagance of his country's costume . . . . Upon his head he wore a black silk handkerchief, the four corners of which hung down his neck behind. An embroidered shirt, a cravat of white jaconet tastefully tied, a blue damask vest, short clothes of crimson velvet, a bright green cloth jacket, with large silver buttons, and shoes of embroidered deer skin, comprised his dress."[3]

Richest of the four Yorba brothers was Bernardo, who lived at his Rancho Cañon de Santa Ana, in Santa Ana Canyon. Bernardo, a home-loving person who seldom left his ranch, had ditches dug from the river to water his orchards and vineyards. He built a water-power grist mill which ground flour and meal. His house, begun in 1834, was one of the largest two-story adobe houses in Southern California.[4]

Although their *vaqueros* (cowboys) and sheep herders must have been familiar with the shores of Newport Bay, these early Mexican owners placed no value upon their beach holdings. It has frequently been noted that the Mexican Dons, who virtually lived in the saddle, were not fishermen as "it is difficult to fish from the back of a horse." Richard Henry Dana, rowing Californians between shore and the brig *Pilgrim*, a sort of floating general store, observed: "These people have no boats of their own."[5] Southern California's seaport in the 1840s and 1850s was San Pedro. Alfred Robinson described the scene when an American "hide drogher" dropped anchor and trading began: "Boats were plying to and fro — launches laden with the variety of our cargo passing to the beach, and men, women, and children crowding upon our decks, partaking in the general excitement. On shore all was confusion. Cattle and carts laden with hides and tallow, *gente de razon*, and Indians, busily employed in the delivery of their produce and receiving in return its value in goods; groups of individuals seated around little bonfires upon the ground, and horsemen racing over the plain in every direction. Thus the day passed; some departing, some arriving; till long after sunset the low white road leading across the plain to the town [Los Angeles] appeared a living panorama."[6]

In 1852 California owners were called upon to prove the legality of their rancho titles by submitting maps, documents, and oral testimony before the United States Land Commission. Both grants adjacent to Newport Bay were confirmed, subsequent surveys being made by Major Henry Hancock. Hancock's map of Rancho San Joaquin, published in 1858, shows the upper bay shaped as it is today, with rough sketches of portions of the state-owned peninsula and marsh islands of the lower bay.[7] Two years after the completion of this first American land survey, Captain William E. Greenwell of the U.S. Coast Survey failed in his attempt to enter Newport Bay to make a preliminary hydrographic examination. The published report of Greenwell's 1860 findings reads as follows:

The lagoon was found to be some five miles long, and separated from the ocean by a narrow strip of sand-beach, over which the heavy southeast and northwest swells wash in every gale. The estuary has a breadth of only a few hundred yards, and receives the river Santa Anna [sic]. Of the entrance to the lagoon Mr. Greenwell reports as follows, "The outlet or mouth is fifty yards in width, with a narrow bar outside, upon which I should judge that twelve feet of water at full tide might be found. Over this bar there is a frightful swell rolling and tumbling at all stages of the tide, making it dangerous to cross in boats of any kind."

With reference to the capacity of the lagoon as a port or harbor, the following remarks are made in the same report: "It may be that the winter rains accumulating in the river and lagoon may deepen the bar so as to admit vessels of thirty or forty tons during winter and spring, and with this in view it will again be examined when the spring opens. At the present time it would be quite impossible to take the schooner Humboldt over the bar, or to cross it in a boat with tents and provisions for a surveying party. There is no anchorage off the entrance, and neither point nor headland to give a lee. The smooth, straight beach, with a trend to the southeast and northwest, gives no protection whatever to vessels from the heavy northwest swell that rolls in with tremendous force."[8]

The *Humboldt* never returned, but there was interest in the unexplored bay. Settlers in San Bernardino and the new town of Anaheim faced hardship and expense in transporting farm products to Phineas T. Banning's new port of Wilmington, up the channel from San Pedro. John S. Hittell mentioned Newport Bay in his *Resources of California*, written in the early 1860s. (Hittell placed the bay in the wrong latitude and gave it some extra length, though his eight miles may have included the Santa Ana River overflow area that stretched toward Huntington Beach). He wrote: "In latitude 34° 38', thirty-five miles southeastward from Los Angeles, is a land-locked estuary about eight miles long and from half a mile to a mile wide. It has not been surveyed and its value for commerce is not known, but there has been some talk lately of using it as a port for some of the adjacent towns. The entrance is not more than ten feet deep, and probably not so deep as that."[9]

Difficult times began in California with floods in the winter of 1861-62. The heaviest rains in the state's recorded history brought destruction from Sacramento to San Diego. Anaheim citizens postponed concern for a port of their own as the Santa Ana River overflowed its banks and sent torrents of water down its ancient western channel to Alamitos Bay, flooding the streets and vineyards of the German colony. Severe drought followed. Seventy-five per cent of Southern California's cattle died during the next three years. J. M. Guinn wrote:

Herds of gaunt, skeleton-like forms moved slowly over the plains in search of food. Here and there, singly or in small groups, poor brutes, too weak to move on, stood motionless with drooping heads, dying. It was a pitiful sight. The loss of cattle during the famine years was fearful. The plains were strewn with their carcasses. In marshy places and around the cienegas where there was a vestige of green the ground was covered with their skeletons; and the traveler for years afterwards was often startled by coming suddenly upon a veritable Golgotha — a place of skulls — the long horns standing out in a defiant attitude, as if defending the fleshless bones.[10]

Like the San Juan Capistrano missionaries of earlier years, rancheros were attracted to the Newport mesa during the drought. José Diego Sepúlveda, a relative of José Andrés Sepúlveda of the San Joaquin Ranch, bought a tract of Yorba land on the mesa and moved with his family to the adobe house on the banks of the Santa Ana River believed to have once served as headquarters of the mission estancia. The river flood plain below was one of the few places where starving cattle could still find pasturage. Diego Sepúlveda's son, Román, later recalled this move "to Newport, for green feed for stock during the dry years." He remembered the happy earlier years when his family, "with the women and girls in hoop skirts, with long pantalettes underneath, and mantillas on their heads, went from their two-story ranch house at Palos Verdes to Los Angeles, via *carreta*, for Holy Week festivities and dances that lasted all night." Now, during the drought years, they lived simply in the small adobe, but "made the journey to San Juan Capistrano for the fiestas, with teams of blooded horses, then in use in place of oxen. This was in the early 1860s and their fine carriage used for the trip was imported from New York and, drawn by the high-stepping horses, made an impressive sight."[11]

But the drought of the 1860s ended the days of the Dons. Even before this blow to the cattle industry, hardships had begun to multiply for the Southern California landowners. Meat prices had fallen in the late 1850s as cattle reached northern California from other sources. In many cases the costs of proving legal titles to land grants, in hearings before the U.S. Land Commission, had been exorbitant. After Americans loaned Spanish-speaking *rancheros* money at high rates of interest, many of them surrendered huge tracts of land for small mortgages they could not repay. Plagued by his debts, colorful José Sepúlveda sold his Rancho San Joaquin in 1864 to Flint, Bixby, Irvine, & Company for $18,000. Captain Salisbury Haley, Sepúlveda's son-in-law, remembered the day when the old Don took the new buyers to show them San Joaquin Bay and the rancho boundaries: "And there we pointed out all these lines. The Red Hill was all in sight; the bay itself, the sheet of water in from the ocean beach [lower bay] — these were all in sight; so that we had a fine prospect for seeing the eastern line of the Santiago de Santa Ana."[12]

Flint, Bixby, and Irvine /4

FLINT, BIXBY, AND IRVINE were wool growers from northern California. As sheep required less pasturage than cattle, while wool brought a high price on markets forced to find substitutes for cotton during and after the Civil War, the sheep industry flourished in Southern California's post-drought years. The new owners stocked the San Joaquin Ranch with thousands of sheep, shipping their wool to San Francisco from Wilmington and from Anaheim's newly opened seaport on Alamitos Bay, Anaheim Landing. Members of the firm were Benjamin Flint, Dr. Thomas Flint, Llewellyn Bixby, and James Irvine. All had come to California in the Gold Rush. Bixby and the Flints were from Maine. After prospering as meat dealers in the mining town of Volcano, they took their carefully guarded gold to the east coast by way of Panama. Traveling west again by rail and wagon, they bought 1880 sheep in Illinois. These, and the lambs born as they went along, the men drove overland all the way to California to begin their wool business in the late 1850s.

James Irvine, a resident of San Francisco, soon became the leader in the operation of the San Joaquin Ranch. Irvine, son of an Anglo-Irish farmer in moderate circumstances, had left his native land at the age of nineteen. After working in New York for two years, he sailed for the California gold fields, via Panama. There he boarded a leaky old 540-ton bark, the *Alexander Von Humboldt* (not to be confused with the Coast Survey schooner *Humboldt*) for a terrible 102-day voyage up the Pacific Coast to San Francisco. Irvine went to the "diggings," but gave up gold seeking in favor of a wholesale grocery business, at which he succeeded. He eventually owned twenty rental houses in San Francisco as well as other real estate.

In 1866 James Irvine married Nettie Rice of Cleveland, Ohio, and brought her west to live in his mansion at the corner of Folsom and Eleventh Streets in San Francisco. In the following year their son, the second James Irvine, was born. Irvine was optimistic about the future of the San Joaquin Ranch in 1868, and wrote in a letter: "We have just built a house costing over $1000. I am sending down furniture so that we shall find it quite comfortable when we go down. A party of us may go down together."[1] At this time the Rancho Santiago de Santa Ana, owned by Yorba and Peralta heirs and others to whom they had sold undivided interests, was being partitioned by court order. Flint, Bixby, and Irvine, who had already added the northerly *Rancho Lomas de Santiago* to their holdings in 1866, now bought the equivalent of 3800 acres of Rancho Santiago de Santa Ana. With this

15

This farmhouse (located where the San Joaquin Golf course is today) served as San Joaquin ranch headquarters from 1868 until 1876. At a meeting held here in the fall of 1870, San Joaquin Bay was renamed Newport Bay.

The first James Irvine (1827-1886) reached California during the Gold Rush. In the 1860s he and his partners bought 108,000 acres of rancho land, including the Newport Bay holdings of José Sepúlveda and a portion of the bay shoreline owned by the Yorbas and their relatives.

California, roads were little more than rutted cowpaths, and rivers were unbridged. The sea was the only satisfactory highway. Years later McFadden recalled his first visit to Newport Bay:

My first arrival in Southern California was by stagecoach on July 5, 1868. At that time there was but one frame house in this country east of the Santa Ana River. That house was then in course of construction on the San Joaquin Ranch, then owned by Irvine, Flint, & Company . . . .

In 1868 while the division of Santa Ana Ranch was under process, the question of the depth of water in the so-called San Joaquin slough became of interest, and through the assistance of a Mr. Goodrich, who was then foreman of the San Joaquin Ranch, I secured the services of an old whaler who was herding a band of sheep for Mr. Goodrich, and who owned or secured a flat bottom boat, and took me over the bar at what he claimed to be mean high tide. I found between 10 and 11 feet on the bar. This was disappointing to all of us, but it was claimed to be more than either Anaheim Landing or San Pedro had at that time.[2]

Although he realized that the bay entrance was too shallow to admit large ocean vessels, McFadden began to dream of a great deep-water port. For the rest of his life he believed that this natural land-locked harbor offered a greater potential than San Pedro, which could be improved only by the construction of large breakwaters. Unlike James Irvine, who had an Irish love of the land and never wished to part with his holdings, McFad-

last addition, awarded to them as a strip three-fourths of a mile wide along the western boundary of Rancho San Joaquin, they owned 108,000 acres of land.

Another purchaser of Rancho Santiago de Santa Ana land was James McFadden, who had bought the equivalent of 4000 acres. McFadden, a young widower from a rural area in the state of New York, had seen the busy port at Wilmington. He wondered about Newport Bay's potential as a seaport. No railroads led to Southern

den wanted to sell his new acreage as small farms and attract population. Eventually, he thought, ocean commerce might be developed for shipments of products from the fertile Santa Ana Valley. James McFadden sold 1200 of his 4000 acres and returned to the east coast. Population would have to come before his dream of an agricultural empire and a seaport could be realized. But the great immigration had begun. Word spread all over the world that the old Spanish and Mexican land grants were being broken up and offered for sale at from two to twelve dollars an acre. Thousands headed for Southern California, by covered wagon and coastal steamer. The "cow counties" were ready for the American farmer and his plow. The Los Angeles *Star* observed on December 19, 1868:

Not a day passes but long trains of emigrant wagons pass through town, from the upper portion of the State, filled with families seeking locations, or rather already *en route* to the homeland selected by a prudent foresight, for the settlement of the family altars. In the vicinity of town, the camps look like a tented field, so numerous are they, where people halt to look them out a location.

The great ranchos having been divided up, induces emigration, and we understand land is offered on such reasonable terms as to hold out superior inducements to settlers. For soil and climate, the southern counties are unequalled in the state. They have long been overlooked, and treated with but very little consideration, if not subject to contumely and contempt, but the time has at last arrived, when their waste places will become habitations and their deserts be made fruitful and blossom as the rose.[3]

NEW PORT BAY, ORANGE CO. CAL.

ON MAY 10, 1869, Leland Stanford drove a gold spike at Promontory, Utah, marking the completion of the first transcontinental railroad. Among those who boarded the train a few months later, bound for San Francisco, were Mr. and Mrs. Harvey Rice of Cleveland, Ohio, parents of young Mrs. James Irvine. Harvey Rice, a distinguished Ohio educator, later described his California trip in a book, *Letters from the Pacific Slope*. He thought it "really a marvel, that we can now traverse a continent in seven or eight days, instead of consuming seven or eight months, as was done with the early emigrants." In San Francisco the Rices visited the Irvines and then left for unpopulated Southern California.

A three-day voyage by paddlewheel steamer took the Rices and James Irvine to San Pedro, where they boarded a small boat for Wilmington and transferred again to the new narrow-gauge railroad leading to Los Angeles. At the Bella Union Hotel Rice found "the best of company and the best accommodations. . . . You will see here but

This timeless photograph of the Newport Upper Bay was made in the 1890s. A river-carved canyon of ancient origin, Newport Upper Bay existed thousands of years before the lower bay (today's Newport Harbor) was formed as the land-locked estuary of the Santa Ana River.

very few ladies, either at the hotels or on the streets. There is just now a rush of adventurers to this point, who are attempting to make fortunes by over-reaching each other." He described Los Angeles as "a unique old town, full of oddities and whimsicalities. The city, with few exceptions, is built in Mexican style, and wears a dilapidated look. . . . The roofs of the houses are generally flat and the walls adobe. . . . It includes within its limits many fine gardens, vineyards, and orange groves. It is emphatically the land of fruits and flowers, always fresh and fascinating." The Rices and James Irvine went by stagecoach to Anaheim, and on to the San Joaquin Ranch in an open carriage. Harvey Rice found that "wool growing is a very profitable business in California," there being forty thousand sheep on the ranch. Of interest is Rice's observation that shark fishermen used San Joaquin Bay, taking boats in and out of its dangerous entrance. He wrote:

On the shore of this bay I saw a camp of Mexican fishermen, who were engaged in manufacturing oil from the carcasses of sharks, which they catch in abundance along the sea coast. The Mexicans make this a profitable business. They go out to sea in small boats, and catch the sharks by harpooning or shooting them, as they rise to the surface in their eagerness to swallow the bait flung to them. When caught, they are towed into the bay, and so great is the number of their skeletons lying about the camp, that the atmosphere throughout the entire vicinity is rendered impure and even offensive.[1]

Rice was surprised to find the country unfenced. "Everybody's herds and flocks graze where they please," he said, "unless watched by herders. It is bewildering to ride through the vast plains of tall grass and wild mustard . . . . Thousands of acres are densely covered with it, and in traveling through it, one is liable to get lost. The country is so level and smooth that you can drive a team in any direction you please. There are but few roads; in many parts of the country nothing more than trails or pathways. It seems to a stranger like an uninhabited land."

But the land was not altogether "uninhabited." Pioneers in covered wagons had crossed the Santa Ana River to buy McFadden land (between Costa Mesa and Santa Ana) and other parcels offered for sale. Most were pleased with the fertile soil and balmy climate of the Santa Ana Valley. Crops were bountiful. Nearby plains, mountains, streams, and ocean waters were a hunter's and fisherman's paradise. But the settlers lacked a market for their bumper harvests of grain and a means of importing lumber, sorely needed for houses, barns, and fences. William Spurgeon, a widowed forty-niner with less than a thousand dollars of capital, decided to establish a new town of Santa Ana, some distance west of the old Mexican settlement of that name. Spurgeon's townsite was covered with yellow-blooming mustard plant. Years later he told

Orange County historian Terry Stephenson about his arrival in 1869:

> No one today [about 1914] can imagine how heavy was that growth of mustard. It was so high that from horseback I could not get an adequate view of the land. I rode around for a while trying to get a better idea of the property I had bought. The mustard was so high that I couldn't see a thing.
>
> I came to a tree from which I believed I could see out over the country. I climbed up into the tree quite a way, perhaps 20 feet. I could look out over the mustard, which appeared like a sea, with here and there sycamore trees rising above it.[2]

Spurgeon pitched his tent nearby. On an October day he hitched up his wagon, crossed the autumn-dry bed of the Santa Ana River, and went down the dusty, rutted twelve-mile trail to Anaheim Landing (moved in 1868 from Alamitos Bay to Bolsa Chiquita). There he bought about $30 worth of lumber with which to build his first store, a small board-and-batten redwood shanty. Then he cleared a road through the mustard to the Anaheim-San Juan Capistrano stagecoach road. It was plain to William Spurgeon, founder of the city of Santa Ana, that he needed better transportation facilities than a wagon road fording a river that would become a raging torrent as soon as winter rains began. Furthermore, the lumber dealers at Anaheim Landing charged dearly for lumber brought by sailing schooners and lightered in from offshore anchorages to *Bolsa Chiquita*. Santa Ana needed a seaport of its own, on the east side of the Santa Ana River. But no one knew yet what the potential of San Joaquin Bay might be. In 1869 the shark fishermen had it all to themselves.

The Steamer *Vaquero* /6

T HE TINY WATERSIDE COMMUNITY of New San Diego boomed in 1869, in response to an announcement that a railroad would be built from Texas to San Diego Harbor. Prospective settlers and speculators streamed in by wagon and steamer to buy lots before prices sky-rocketed as they had in San Francisco. While newcomers lived in covered wagons or spread blankets on the ground, Captain Samuel Sumner Dunnells, proprietor of the town's small wooden hotel, turned crowds away. "Start the hammers," the San Diego *Union* admonished. "Keep the nicely furnished rooms and parlors for the women and children and fix temporary rooms for the gentlemen."[1]

San Diego historian Jerry MacMullen has described Captain Dunnells as a "fine, full-bearded man and as typical a Down East shipmaster as one could wish." The pleasant and obliging Mrs. Dunnells was "cook and chambermaid, famous for her biscuits."[2] But Dunnells, a newcomer himself, grew restless as he looked at the beautiful waters of San Diego Harbor. He had grown up on the shores of Penobscot Bay on the coast of Maine, gone to sea as a boy of 17, served as a Great Lakes ship captain, and sailed around Cape Horn to join the California gold rush. After years of operating a general merchandise store in the gold country, he had opened the New San Diego Hotel. In his spare time he was building a boat, "the yacht *Vigorous*." Before long Captain Dunnells leased his hotel and began carrying freight and passengers up and down the harbor.

Optimism about the future of New San Diego had spread to the waterfront. Wharves were being built to welcome the large ships that would surely arrive once the railroad was built. A tugboat would be useful to tow sailing vessels across shallow areas in San Diego Bay. With hopeful enthusiasm Captain Dunnells went to San Francisco where he bought the wood-burning *Vaquero*, a flat-bottomed sturdy little steamer built especially for shallow-water navigation. Dr. Samuel Merritt, founder of the city of Oakland and later owner of the *Casco* on which Robert Louis Stevenson went to the South Seas, had given the boat a festive launching on September 9, 1865:

> The stern-wheeler *Vaquero*, built by Mr. Allen, for Dr. Merritt, for freighting between Oakland and Clinton on the eastern shore of the bay and this city [San Francisco] was launched at South Beach between Second and Third Streets, yesterday afternoon. The tide serving, the steamer was launched at half past two p.m., a half-hour earlier than had been

announced, somewhat to the disappointment of a large number of people who had started down to see her take to the water. She glided gracefully from the ways and entered the briny element without disaster or detention of any kind whatever. A light collation was served on board after the launch and before she reached the wharf.

The dimensions of this neat little craft are as follows: length of keel 100 feet, length of deck 120 feet, breadth of beam 25 feet. Her freight capacity is about [105] tons, and her engines are of 80 horse power. Running light she will draw but about twelve inches. Her wheel is decked over so as to give quite a lengthy promenade deck, and she presents a very neat appearance generally.[3]

The *Vaquero* was "the earliest vessel of steam propulsion to be permanently located in San Diego."[4] At first Dunnells used her for towing, carrying freight, and pleasure excursions. Men, women, and children crowded aboard for Sunday and holiday trips, reporting that "our bold skipper of the *Vaquero* .... knows the head of the bay like a book." On one occasion the captain took along a band of musicians to entertain passengers on a camping and fishing trip to Los Coronados Islands. Another time he offered a prize of $5 for the largest fish caught and $2.50 for the smallest. A satisfied excursionist wrote: "Captain Dunnells is highly spoken of for his attention to all on board and his efforts to contribute to the pleasure and comfort of the trip. He knows how to run a steamboat as well as how to keep a hotel."[5]

Dunnells found other uses for the *Vaquero* as months went by without the arrival of a railroad or fleets of ships that needed towing into San Diego Harbor. Most of the new settlers had little money, employment was scarce, and meager food supplies unloaded by the one coastal steamship company were expensive. The town faced an acute grain shortage. Settlers had brought horses, cows, and chickens. Several stagecoach companies had terminals in San Diego, requiring large amounts of hay and other feed for their horses and mules. Thus it was that the little river boat became an ocean freight vessel.

Early in April, 1870, the *Vaquero* transported sixty tons of hay and grain from Anaheim Landing, returning a week later for another load. While continuing in this hay and grain trade she made other ocean voyages, taking fifty tons of coal to a British vessel stranded off the coast of Baja California. When summer came she carried seven tons of wire and 1700 spindly poles for the first telegraph line between San Diego and San Juan Capistrano. Along the way the poles were floated to shore, "a dangerous service, performed by Captain S. S. Dunnells."[6] During the next few weeks the *Vaquero* picked up cargoes of salt and firewood on the Mexican coast and brought several loads of hay and grain from Wilmington. Her heaviest cargoes were about ninety tons.

Wilmington and Anaheim Landing were fierce rivals. Wilmington, the larger port, had the advantage of its 22-mile-long railroad to Los Angeles. But the energetic Germans of Anaheim were also competent managers of a shipping business. By-passing Los Angeles, in 1870 a town of 5,728 people with a farming economy similar to their own, they had built up a direct maritime trade with San Francisco. Los Angeles citizens were concerned about Anaheim Landing's wagon route which attracted shipments from Riverside and San Bernardino that might otherwise have gone to Wilmington. An impressive number of vessels called at Anaheim Landing, twelve miles from Anaheim and near today's city of Seal Beach. Ships anchored a mile out at sea, where they unloaded freight and passengers onto barge-like lighters that were drawn by cables to the wharf and warehouse inside Bolsa Chiquita inlet. Among sidewheel steamers making regular stops at Anaheim Landing in 1870 were the *Orizaba*, *Pacific*, *California*, *William Tabor*, *Oriflamme*, and *Mohongo*, as well as a number of lumber schooners.

Captain Dunnells learned of the transportation difficulties faced by settlers in and near the new towns of Santa Ana and Tustin. They had corn and other products they could not sell. They needed lumber, a "cash" item at Anaheim Landing. Few pioneers had money. Barter was the usual method of exchange, even at William Spurgeon's store. San Diego needed grain, and had finally built up a lumber surplus. William A. Abbott, a friend of Captain Dunnells, had imported a yard full that he could not sell. The two men, and a third named Daniel Dorman, decided to trade San Diego lumber for Santa Ana Valley farm products. There was one unanswered question — could a ship enter San Joaquin Bay?

Captain Samuel Sumner Dunnells (1824-1903) was a Maine sea captain, forty-niner, storekeeper, hotel owner, master of the steamer *Vaquero*, and port pilot of San Diego Harbor.

The steamer *Vaquero*, a flat-bottomed river sternwheeler built in San Francisco in 1865, was this type of vessel.

The first edition of George Davidson's *Pacific Coast Pilot* had come off the presses a few months earlier. It contained no sailing directions for the Santa Ana River estuary, only dire warnings based on Greenwell's 1860 experiences with the *Humboldt*: "On the bar there is a very heavy break at all stages of the tide, rendering it dangerous to cross in boats of any kind. There is said to be no safe anchorage off the entrance, and the low straight beach, with a trend nearly east and west, affords no protection whatever. . . . The attempts to pass the bar were, in all cases, attended with risk, and the entrance may for general purposes, be regarded as impracticable."[7] Davidson's warnings were wise, but Captain Dunnells was a pilot of exceptional skill.

Sect. X.
U.S. COAST SURVEY
Carlile P. Patterson Supdt.
TOPOGRAPHY IN VICINITY OF
NEWPORT BAY
CALIFORNIA
1875   Surveyed by
A.W. Chase Assist. U.S.C.S.
Scale 20000   E. Ellicott Sub Assist. U.S.C.S.
F.A. Lawson Aid

Register Nº 1392.

Map based on the 1875
topographic survey,
showing Newport Bay at
low tide. Darkly shaded
areas are marshlands,
lightly shaded portions
are tidelands, and dots
along the peninsula
represent large sand
dunes.

Newport
Landing

Road to Santa Ana and Anaheim

P A C I F I C   O C E A N

A New Port /7

UNNELLS, ABBOTT, and DORMAN loaded the *Vaquero* with 5000 shingles and 5000 feet of lumber from the San Diego lumber yard. They steamed out of the harbor — bound, supposedly, for Anaheim Landing. Their real destination was San Joaquin Bay. An exchange of lumber for hay and grain appeared feasible if they could enter the estuary and find a satisfactory landing place. The *Vaquero* was an ideal ship for the purpose. In the bay entrance, where a sailing ship might meet disaster, her motors would give speed and stability. If stranded on a mudflat or sandbar she had only to put her big sternwheel into reverse and back off. She could negotiate sharp turns and needed no wharf at which to land as her bow could be nudged against the shore.

On September 10, 1870, the sound of engines was heard for the first time across the marshes of the Santa Ana River estuary. The Corona del Mar hillsides and the Newport mesa would have been brown and gold in the September sunlight as the *Vaquero* made her way safely through the "impracticable" entrance and along the south side of the marsh that later became Balboa Island, turning north at Bay Island to pass the tip of the future Lido Isle and enter the upper bay. Continuing northward she carefully followed the channel, making a number of sharp turns as she passed the narrows and reached the then-deep basin at the head of the upper bay. Dunnells, Abbott, and Dorman landed at a point on the shore beneath a freshwater spring known since Indian times. Only eight miles from Santa Ana, it would have been a good place for a wharf.

But the many turns along the way had been difficult for the *Vaquero*. Captain Dunnells and his friends returned to the shark fishermen's beach at the southwest end of the upper bay, beneath Castaways Bluff. They landed their lumber and constructed a small temporary wharf. Word traveled fast. Before long James Irvine was on his way from San Francisco. The McFadden brothers, James and Robert, crossed the continent to San Francisco by train and made the last part of their trip by stagecoach. The Los Angeles *Star* made an exciting announcement:

"NEW LANDING. The steamer *Vaquero* landed a cargo last Saturday at a point east of the Santa Ana River. . . . It is said that a good landing can easily be made at the place referred to. If this is a fact, it is of great importance to those settling on the fertile lands east of the Santa Ana River, across which the road to Anaheim Landing passes, and which is nearly impassable during the rainy season."[1]

James McFadden has described the historic meeting at the San Joaquin ranch house, at which the new port received its name: "Until 1870 the present bay of Newport was known as the San Joaquin slough. In 1870 the name 'Newport' was suggested by a Mrs. Perkins, who, with her husband, was in the employ of Irvine, Flint & Company, living at their house on the San Joaquin ranch, and this suggestion was accepted by James Irvine, Sr., Benjamin Flint, my brother Robert, and myself, all of whom were stopping at this new frame house at the time." The Los Angeles *Star* announced the new name, but offered no congratulations. *Newport* was a "threatened calamity"[3] that would join Anaheim Landing in drawing business away from Wilmington.

Flint, Bixby, Irvine & Company applied for a wharf franchise at the shark fishermen's beach and, on October 14, 1870, filed maps of two new townsites, *Newport* and *Wallula*, each to contain sixteen lots. Newport was located on the west banks of the upper bay, in today's Baycrest subdivision. Wallula was on Castaways Bluff, just above the location Dunnells had chosen for his landing. When the ranch owners' wharf franchise was granted in November, they made Dunnells a proposition for use of the wharf they planned to build, but the captain declined.[4] Apparently Dunnells and B. G. Perkins, interim manager of the San Joaquin Ranch, did not get along with one another. Saying only that he wanted a landing of his own,[5] Captain Dunnells moved his lumber 200 feet down the beach, applied to the Los Angeles County supervisors for a second franchise, and began to build a warehouse.

John Cubbon, a young Englishman who had left San Diego because of disappointment in the boom, arrived to work at the new landing. He built "a levee to keep the tide water away from the lumber." Next he graded a trail up the bluff that a Portuguese fisherman, Manuel, had been using for his pony cart, and went off to the Santa Ana River bed to cut willow firewood for the *Vaquero*.[6] William Tedford, the first farmer to plow ground on the McFadden lands, rode horseback down to the landing and arranged to sell Captain Dunnells a load of potatoes to take to San Diego. Returning to his farm he marked out the future road across the mesa "by gathering dry cattle bones [remaining from the drought of 1863-64] and placing them in piles on prominent places along the way to designate the course back to the steamer."[7]

Dunnells' wharf franchise was granted after a delay of several months, but there seemed to be little potential for the *Vaquero* in a San Diego-Newport Bay trade. Business declined all over Southern California because of a drought in the winter of 1870-71. Additional lumber for the yard at the landing, now managed by William A. Abbott, would have to be brought from northern California. Even if his relations with the San Joaquin Ranch owners had been friendly, Dunnells could not have taken their wool to San Francisco, the only west coast market for it. Firewood for the *Vaquero's* engine was expensive, and she often sailed in ballast from San Diego to Newport, Anaheim Landing, or Wilmington. With his finances in the red, Captain Dunnells steamed off to San Pedro where he spent the summer of 1871, probably using the *Vaquero* as a freight boat during the construction of the first small breakwater there.

In the meantime, a sailing vessel had entered Newport Bay. In May the schooner *Golden Gate*, "laden with fence posts, sailed from off the briny ocean right into Newport, below Santa Ana. No soundings were taken and no difficulty was experienced."[8] Four months later, in early September, the schooner *Solano*, with a cargo of lumber from Stewart's Point, went aground on the bar in the entrance to Newport Bay. A telegram to Wilmington for help brought no response. A month later the ship was still on the bar. The Anaheim *Gazette* stated: "The schooner *Solano* is still on the inside bar at Newport, and not likely to leave there except in pieces. Part of her bottom is gone, also the rudder, and she proves to be much more damaged than was at first supposed. Every effort has been made to save her, without avail."[9]

Three weeks later the *Vaquero*, missing from the local scene for months, steamed into the bay. Captain Dunnells promised to bring help to the stricken *Solano*. First he obtained a load of hay and grain at Anaheim Landing, gave the German proprietors a promissory note, and went off to San Diego. He returned to Newport with "apparatus for getting the *Solano* on the ways, where she will be repaired."[10] After rescue operations that took several weeks, Captain Dunnells towed the *Solano* to the landing. By Christmas, 1871, the schooner was afloat again. Dunnells returned to San Diego, his vessel laden with hay, grain, and "a lot of wine" from Anaheim.[11] But the captain's financial picture was no brighter. He owed $487.95 to the grain merchants at Anaheim Landing and $551.72 to an Anaheim hardware store.

Considering the pride that Anaheim Landing took in its San Bernardino trade, Dunnells' next move was probably unwise. He announced early in April, 1872, that he would explore the coastline to find a new landing for San Bernardino. Immediately afterward, his Anaheim creditors went to their lawyers. Dunnells faced two lawsuits, both demanding that the *Vaquero* be seized and sold. On April 18, 1872 the San Diego sheriff received a writ of attachment and seized the sternwheeler.[12] There is no evidence that the Maine sea captain ever set foot aboard her again. Six weeks later the sheriff released the *Vaquero* to Captain Dunnells' partner, William A. Abbott, manager of Newport Landing. As "Captain Abbott" he took the ship to Newport Bay, apparently intending to use her as a lighter to transport cargoes from ocean vessels into the bay. But the barley crop in the Santa Ana Valley was abundant that year, and the overworked *Vaquero* took several loads to San Diego. On July 20 she left San Diego for Newport but returned disabled, her boilers leaking and fires out. In seven days of repairs she was "thoroughly refitted and put in seaworthy condition."[13]

Early in August the *Vaquero* sailed out of San Diego Harbor for the last time. She continued past Newport, Anaheim Landing, and Wilmington — making her way up the coast to San Francisco. She spent the remainder of her days on the inland waters of San Francisco Bay, until taken out of service in the year 1881. Captain Dunnells returned to managing his hotel, but soon built another sailing sloop. During the lean years that followed the San Diego boom he supplemented his income by fishing, drying his catch, and shipping it to San Francisco. For more than a decade he served as one of the two official pilots for the port of San Diego. His son, Edwin, succeeded him as port pilot. San Diego remembers him as a "good citizen." He is remembered also as the captain of the *Vaquero*, a small river steamer that went to sea more than a hundred years ago and found a "new port."

The McFadden brothers, *circa* 1900. Seated, left to right, James, Archie, and John; standing, Robert. James McFadden (1833-1919), Santa Ana's leading pioneer, played a prominent role in the formation of Orange County. With his brother Robert (1845-1922), he carried on maritime shipping enterprises at Newport from 1875 until 1899. John McFadden, a partner with James and Robert in the operation of Newport Landing from 1876 until 1878, was later a Santa Ana hardware merchant and an early mayor of the city. Archie, last of the four brothers to move from the family farm in Delaware County, New York, became an Orange County rancher.

The McFadden Brothers /8

COMMERCIAL ACTIVITY at Newport Landing ceased after the last departure of the *Vaquero* in the summer of 1872. Captain Abbott left the small wharf and warehouse and moved to Santa Ana. Although Hubert Wakeham, a settler on the McFadden lands, noted in his journal that a schooner went aground in the Newport Bay entrance in 1873, there is no other evidence of renewed shipping business until 1875. In the meantime, a small population and lack of capital hindered the growth of the area which Newport Landing might have served. Anaheim Landing, however, enjoyed its greatest prosperity in the fall of 1872 when the Anaheim *Gazette* observed: "From thirty to forty teams per day arrive and depart with loads of export and import and we believe as high as seventy teams have been at the Landing in a single day this season."[1]

Robert McFadden, younger brother of James McFadden, no doubt dreamed that some day Newport Landing would be as prosperous as Anaheim Landing, but progress on the east side of the river was slow. After the meeting at the San Joaquin ranch house in the fall of 1870 when Newport received its new name, he had remained at Santa Ana while James returned to the east coast. Robert's job was to sell his older brother's acreage at prices ranging from eight to fifteen dollars an acre.

So few buyers appeared that he went to work clearing brush on a neighbor's land. When he and a settler, Jerome Porter, decided to start a dairy, they found no good fresh water although shallow wells of brackish water were plentiful. Borrowing equipment, the two young men drilled into the ground with a four-inch pipe and soon had a tall fountain of artesian water bubbling from the top of the pipe. Before long numerous wells tapped the Santa Ana Valley's bounteous underground reserves of pure water.

On one occasion McFadden traded some of his brother's land for a few hogs. John Cubbon, who had helped Dunnells and Abbott at the landing, joined him in a venture to cure ham and bacon. When the meat was ready, they could find no market. Cubbon finally loaded up a wagon and took it to the mining camps of Arizona but never collected all the money due him. Remembering pioneer days Robert McFadden once told Terry Stephenson: "Farmers here had a lot harder time in those early years than people who came in later years could imagine. The outlook was far from bright."[2] When Cubbon contracted typhoid fever, a doctor rode muleback from Anaheim to prescribe for him, and McFadden took care of his sick friend.

Although Flint, Bixby, and Irvine's platted settlement

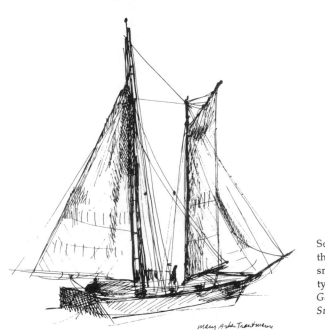

Some of the early lumber schooners that entered Newport Bay were small two-masted vessels of this type. Among them were the *Golden Gate, Solano, Mose,* and *Susie.*

Mary Arba Trautmann

"Nearly every farmhouse kept a boat turned up against the shady side of the barn so that they were able to get out if flood came. The floods never had any current to them, the water just raised up from the river and stayed there till it gradually drained out and cleared off again."[3] Most of the early residents of Gospel Swamp were devout people, mainly Methodists and Mormons, who held frequent prayers meetings. It was said that the head of every household was capable of delivering a sermon, but the Reverend Isaac Hickey was the best known local preacher. Camp meetings held on the banks of the Santa Ana River were religious in nature, but also provided the pioneers with sociability and entertainment.

In 1874 Santa Ana began to show signs of prosperity. New houses and frame buildings appeared. A visitor to William Spurgeon's store thought it looked like a mining camp trading post. He saw "two such sweet girls buying ribbons, and a man from Tustin City buying six sacks of flour. . . . Lying around were loose blankets, whips, guns, tea, coffee, tinware, treacle, perfumery, books, stationery . . . pickles, blacking, pins, needles, and yellow soap."[4] Out in front stood wagons full of hides and wool. Newport Bay was a frequent topic of conversation at Spurgeon's store, favorite gathering place of farmers from Gospel Swamp and other areas. According to rumor, the McFadden brothers, James and Robert, were planning to reopen the landing. The U.S. Coast Survey was ready at last to make the long-delayed hydrographic survey. A Captain Dabney steamed into the bay aboard the survey ship *San Luis,* took a few preliminary soundings, inspected the Newport bar, and announced that small steamers could cross it easily. But who had a "small steamer?" If anyone could produce such a boat, the pros-

of Newport remained a "paper town" that never materialized, the name was given to a settlement (now Greenville) that grew up on the McFadden lands north of Costa Mesa. Some of its early settlers were the Tedford and Wakeham families. This farming community appears on many early maps as Newport, but the local farmers called it "Gospel Swamp," a name also given later to peatlands across the Santa Ana River. The original Gospel Swamp was not a swamp at all, but one of the most fertile agricultural regions in the world, producing bumper crops of corn, pumpkins, and alfalfa. It was, however, subject to flooding during the rainy season. Arthur J. McFadden, son of Robert McFadden, recalls, pects would be bright indeed. The Anaheim *Gazette* painted a rosy future: "Newport — 'yes, sir!' and a fashionable place it will be yet. For only 8 miles from this embryo city [Santa Ana] is the harbor of Newport, at the mouth of the Santa Ana River, where there is a wharf and warehouse all ready to be used for storage. Here then is an opening for some enterprising capitalist to start a lumber yard, where the entire valley can be supplied as the roads are good and free from sand. Here also the products of the valley may be shipped cheaper than at other points. The agricultural resources of this beautiful valley are really very great. Wheat, barley, and corn flourish in the greatest luxuriance, and pumpkins actually grow to the size of 228 pounds!"[5]

It was a warning to the proprietors of Anaheim Landing, who sent the Wilson brothers, two Scandinavian fishermen, to lease the wharf and warehouse from William A. Abbott. The Wilsons were to rent boats and tackle, while keeping away any "enterprising capitalist" who might decide to open a shipping business at Newport. But there was already an enterprising capitalist at work. James McFadden had returned to California from New York, bringing his second wife and two small daughters. From Santa Ana pioneer Thomas Casad he bought 1,800 acres of land north of his original purchase of 4,000 acres, and a two-story brick house that was to be his home for nearly four decades.

Turning his attention to Newport Landing, James McFadden applied to the state of California for a patent to the twenty acres of beach on which the Dunnells and Abbott warehouse had been built, hoping the site could be bought as "swamp and overflow" land, then available from the state for a dollar an acre. He won the friendship of C. E. French, manager of the San Joaquin Ranch, and a pledge of cooperation if he could establish a landing on Newport Bay. In San Francisco McFadden ordered a "small steamer" capable of making the dangerous voyages from northern California lumber ports to Newport Bay. George S. and Charles A. Hooper, San Francisco shippers and lumber mill owners, agreed to supervise the construction of the new vessel. Builders were the well-known Dickie brothers, John and James. The *Newport* was to be a 331-ton freighter, built of wood and equipped with sails as well as with a single screw engine. Capable of a speed of 7.5 knots, the ship was to be 133.5 feet long, 25.5 feet wide, and 9.9 feet deep.[6] The *Newport* was one of the first of those strange but useful little vessels called steam schooners.

In his *Ships of the Redwood Coast* (Stanford University Press, 1945) Jerry MacMullen describes the steam schooner as "a type of ocean-going vessel which became a dominant factor in the development of the rich timberlands and which played a vital part in the growth of the state. It was small because it had to be; you just don't go puttering around through breakers and into wind-swept dogholes on the Mendocino shore in a liner or a 10,000-ton freighter . . . . It is dog-hole work, a doghole, in case you do not know, being an indentation in a rocky coastline, of course really bigger than an opening into which a dog might crawl, squirm around, and crawl out again, but not much . . . . The little ship which was born to take on the job of getting millions of board feet of California redwood to the markets of the world was the steam schooner — a thing as uniquely Californian as the Golden Gate, Olvera Street, or the redwoods themselves."

The *Newport* was not to be ready until late in the summer of 1875. While waiting for her completion, James McFadden needed fence lumber (barbed wire was not yet in general use) as he wished to begin feeding cattle. The Hooper brothers agreed to send down 100,000 board feet of lumber on their schooner, *Mose*, from the northern California port of Trinidad. If her skipper, Captain Brown, successfully crossed the Newport bar, the McFaddens were to send the *Mose* back with a cargo of barley at five dollars a ton. If not, they would raft the lumber ashore. In the meantime, the U.S. Coast Survey work at Newport Bay had begun. The McFaddens welcomed the survey party, but wanted to get rid of Anaheim Landing's Wilson brothers as soon as possible. John Cubbon went to William A. Abbott and bought the wharf and warehouse for the McFaddens, but the Wilsons refused to leave. John Cubbon later described their departure:

"One day several of us got together . . . and went down. The Wilsons were away fishing, and we had no trouble with the man in charge. We laid out a sail on the flat and dumped all their belongings on it. When the Wilsons got back they were fighting mad. One of them started to bring things back into the warehouse, and I stopped him. He grabbed a cross-cut saw and rushing at me swung it down on the top of my head. I'll never forget how big those saw teeth looked as they were coming down. Of course I dodged, and that is all that kept me from being killed. The saw teeth caught on my hat and shoulder, and I wasn't hurt."[7] In the ensuing fracas one Wilson brother was knocked unconscious and the other thrown into the water. When the Scandinavians were conscious and dry again, they departed. Newport Landing, also called McFadden Landing, was ready for the arrival of the *Mose*.

Captain Brown brought the two-masted, flat-bottomed, centerboard scow into the bay by kedging, and unloaded her cargo of lumber. Robert McFadden remembered: "We did not get to use much of that first load ourselves. Farmers came in from all around. First, one would want enough to build a corral, then another would want enough to put up a shed, and they all needed the lumber so bad that I sold quite a lot of it."[8] Other small schooners joined the *Mose* on the Trinidad-Newport run in the spring and early summer of 1875, among them the *Susie, Glenarm, Teutonia, Alice,* and *Golden Gate.* A typical return cargo for the *Mose,* requiring from two to three weeks for the voyage to San Francisco, was "1416 sacks corn, 615 sacks barley, 90 sacks beans, 61 sacks wheat, 250 bales wool." This schooner trade, carried on while the *Newport* was under construction, was not altogether satisfactory. The ships were small, costs were high, and "it was dangerous to cross the bar with sail."[9]

Hooper Brothers owned a small pioneer version of the steam schooner, the *Twin Sisters,* that they sent to Newport in May, as the work of the U.S. Coast Survey came to an end. This ship was described as "a small but beautiful vessel . . . . the forerunner of one being built for Mr. McFadden, of Newport, at an expense of some twenty thousand dollars."[10] The *Twin Sisters* entered Newport Bay in rough weather and promptly went on the bar. Robert McFadden blamed the captain, who had ignored signals from shore to drop anchor and wait. It was more than a month before the ship was floated "by the aid of wine casks, etc." During the first months the McFaddens operated the landing, Captain Brown also once ran the *Mose* aground on a sandbar. In order to lighten the vessel and get her afloat he "threw off a lot of grain" at the expense of the McFaddens.[11]

As the *Newport* neared completion, the McFadden brothers, aided by Gospel Swamp farmers, graded the wagon trail across the mesa to Santa Ana and enlarged the wharf and warehouse. The new steamer entered the bay on September 3, 1875, five years after the first arrival of the *Vaquero*. San Joaquin Ranch manager Charles E. French prepared the press release:

> The McFaddens' new steamer arrived at Newport Harbor on last Friday, with a cargo of one hundred and fifty thousand feet of lumber. The arrival was quite an important event in the history of Southern Los Angeles County. The immense number of people in the large farming section, of which Newport is the natural outlet, are of course deeply interested in having facilities for the shipment of their produce.
>
> On Sunday last, notwithstanding the counter-attraction of the Camp Meeting, over 100 persons visited Newport for the purpose of inspecting the vessel and exchanging congratulations on the auspicious event.
>
> The vessel is named *Newport* and is commanded by Captain Pierce, recently first mate on the *Orizaba*, and who is acquainted with every nook and cranny in the coast from San Francisco to San Diego. The vessel . . . .when loaded draws only 7½ feet of water. She can carry 1000 head of sheep, or take a cargo of 1000 bales of wool. The vessel is admirably fitted up and has several staterooms for the accommodation of passengers.

Steam schooners were equipped with engines but also rigged fore and aft. The *Twin Sisters* was probably a remodeled sailing vessel, but the McFadden brothers, *Newport* was one of the first pioneer vessels designed and built as a ship of this type.

> The engines and machinery are of the most approved pattern. It is expected to make the trip from San Francisco to Newport about every two weeks. The warehouses at Newport have been for some time filled with grain. Some idea of the vast progress being made by the region . . . can be gathered from the fact that on Monday last, 80 teams were loaded with lumber at Newport; in fact most of the cargo of 150,000 feet had been engaged two months ago.[12]

FOR A QUARTER OF A CENTURY after their re-opening of Newport Landing in 1875, James and Robert McFadden were the leaders in the shipping business along the coast of Orange County (separated from Los Angeles County in 1889). For a time James and Robert were joined in the Newport enterprise by a third brother, John, later mayor of Santa Ana. The brothers were three of eleven children born to John and Effie McFadden, thrifty Scottish farmers who had settled in Delaware County, New York. James and John had taught school, but all the brothers remained interested in agriculture throughout their lives. James McFadden, the eldest, a man of "endless energy and patriotism,"[1] was destined to become Santa Ana's most influential and powerful citizen. With many friends throughout the state, he was an active participant in California politics although he never ran for public office. Of less than medium height and always impeccably dressed, James McFadden was "quiet in speech and demeanor, yet quick and decisive in action."[2] He was the leader in the maritime enterprise at Newport Landing and handled the promotional details. Robert, tall and rugged, supervised

The McFadden brothers' steamer *Newport*, photographed in the 1870s or 1880s at a northern California lumber port.

the landing where he lived until 1884, working out of doors with sailors and longshoremen. John was business manager and accountant.

The *Newport* entered the bay every two weeks on the highest tides. She brought cargoes of lumber from the scenic but treacherous rocky inlet at Trinidad, and carried meat, grain, produce, wool, and farm animals to San Francisco. The year 1876 was a prosperous one, bringing the crest of California's boom of the seventies. Thousands of new settlers arrived. Land prices rose dramatically. Adding to Newport Landing's success was the demise of Anaheim Landing, deserted by coastal steamers after the completion in 1875 of the Southern Pacific's spur railroad from Los Angeles to Anaheim.

With its seaport in operation, Santa Ana soon boasted four general stores, two hotels, a restaurant, blacksmith shops, two drug stores, livery stables, three saloons, and other businesses in rough wooden buildings adjacent to its main intersection. But when the Santa Ana Valley *News* declared that Newport Bay was as fine a harbor as Charleston, South Carolina, the Anaheim *Gazette* replied with a little friendly banter. If Newport really had such a fine harbor, why had it been kept a secret for so long? "If a fine class of steamers can cross the Newport bar, why don't they do it?"[3] Indeed, editorialized the *Gazette*, the Newport entrance had an average high tide depth of less than eight feet, making it doubtful "whether as great risks are taken by any steamer on the coast as the one running in and out of Newport."

In describing his admittedly risky business, James McFadden recalled that the *Newport* "drew about nine feet of water loaded, and could only cross the bar every two weeks on extreme high tides. By keeping a close watch on the bar by constant soundings we were fairly successful although the business was extremely hazardous on account of shifting quicksands and the lack of water on the bar."[4] Robert, associated with the day-to-day operation of the landing, was "thrown out in the water a good many times, and swamped many times on the bar."[5] Eventually the McFaddens built two lighters. Guided by poles, these barge-like boats were floated in and out of the bay with the tides to unload and load sailing vessels anchored in the ocean outside the entrance, and also the *Newport* when there was not enough water on the bar for her to cross it. Lumber was often thrown overboard, and floated ashore through the surf. The McFaddens maintained a lumber yard on the bluffs at Rocky Point (Corona del Mar) where they stacked the water-soaked wood to dry before shipping it inland on mule and horse-drawn lumber wagons.

The winter of 1876-77 was a dry one, resulting in drought, depression, and the collapse of the boom of the seventies. As business began to drop off, the McFaddens faced an additional worry in the form of a dispute with James Irvine, who had absorbed his partners' interests on September 27, 1876 and become sole owner of the San Joaquin Ranch. In that same year James McFadden received his patent to the 20-acre beach on which the landing was located, having applied for it in 1874 as "swamp and overlow" land. Irvine claimed that McFadden had made the application as an agent of Flint, Bixby, Irvine & Company, and that the landing site belonged to the San Joaquin Ranch.

Settlers already resented James Irvine's refusal to grant the Southern Pacific Railroad a right of way across his ranch. When the San Francisco capitalist (who owned virtually all the mainland shoreline of the upper and lower bays) threatened to evict the McFaddens from the Newport Landing tidelands, the Anaheim *Gazette* published a Tustin citizen's complaint:

> An attempt is now being made to float the ranch line . . . over the *tide lands*, the title to which was obtained by various parties under state law governing tide lands in California . . . .
>
> Now, the object of the present owner of the ranch is to dispossess the legitimate owners of this tide land, under the plea that it belongs to the rancho and consequently close the harbor; for there is no doubt, reasoning by analogy, but that the same policy would be pursued in regard to the harbor, should the present owner obtain possession of it, as has been pursued in regard to the rancho lands. Why is it that we have no railroad here today? Simply because the "whole hog or none" Policy governs the management of these lands, and the right of way cannot be obtained. Why is it that he wishes to close our harbor? Simply to gratify a little personal spite, he proposes to ruin the only outlet for produce of our whole people.[6]

Extended litigation between James McFadden and James Irvine was finally ended on January 21, 1880. Judge Ignacio Sepúlveda decided that McFadden had no right to the landing beach, and that it belonged to James Irvine. Irvine, described by historian Robert Glass Cleland as known in his business affairs "for sagacity, sound judgment, sense of fairness and justice" and his "exactitude even in the most trivial transactions," was by no means insensitive to public opinion. No railroad crossed the San Joaquin Ranch as long as he lived, but he reached an understanding with the McFadden brothers after the end of the lawsuit in 1880. They were permitted to maintain the landing on the Irvine beach, and to lease Irvine land on the bluff above, where they built a large three-level warehouse.

The McFaddens' lawsuit with James Irvine was not the only difficulty that arose in their operation of the landing. On April 8, 1878, the *Newport* arrived, too heavily laden to cross the bar. A small boat was lowered, carrying the mate and three sailors who were to wait outside the surf for a line that would be floated to them through the entrance, from a lighter inside the bay. They were to tie the line to their kedge anchor and drop it into the water. Crewmen on the lighter would then pull on the line to draw their craft through the entrance and out to the *Newport*. Instead of waiting beyond the surf for the line to reach him, the mate took the boat directly into the breakers, where it capsized. Captain Pierce leaped into a second boat with two additional crew members and rowed to the rescue, but he met the same fate. Seven men floundered helplessly in the entrance swells. James McMillan, a Scottish sailor employed at the landing, left the lighter with a small boat and rescued two

crew members, one of them the mate who had caused the trouble. But five men, including the *Newport's* capable Captain Pierce, were drowned.

James McFadden, William Spurgeon, and others had contributed $10,100 to the Southern Pacific Railroad, which extended its rails to Santa Ana late in 1877. McFadden felt betrayed when the railroad promptly opened a rate war against the *Newport*. At the same time Los Angeles merchants, victims of collusion between the railroad and steamship line that raised their freight rates, turned to McFadden, Southern California's only independent shipper, for help. He rented a "mud wharf" warehouse at Wilmington and carried cargo on the *Newport* from Los Angeles to San Francisco at three dollars a ton. The Pacific Coast Steamship Company announced that it would carry grain free on days the *Newport* left port, and the railroad also lowered its Los Angeles rates. Unable to operate profitably out of either Newport Bay or Wilmington, James McFadden lost $6000 while trying to keep his business alive. On November 1, 1878, he gave up the battle and sold the *Newport* to the Pacific Coast Steamship Company.

It was an amicable settlement. McFadden transferred his favorable shipping contracts with Santa Ana and San Bernardino farmers to Goodall, Nelson, and Perkins, agents for the steamship company. They, in turn, agreed to bring the *Newport* to the landing every two weeks, but did not take her to northern California lumber ports. Instead she became a tramp steamer, putting in at every port between San Francisco and Newport Bay. Robert McFadden continued to operate the landing, depending now upon smaller supplies of lumber brought by schooners that anchored outside the entrance, transferr-

ing cargoes to lighters or floating them ashore. John McFadden left the shipping business and moved to Santa Ana, where he became a pioneer hardware dealer. James, who grieved all his life over the loss of Captain Pierce and the four sailors, turned his attention to his large farm, wholesale meat business, and real estate interests. He still believed in Newport's future as a great harbor, but his first attempt to build maritime trade had been a disappointment.

The Steamer Newport

Warehouse and chute at Newport Landing. Sacks of grain were sent down a hinged chute, directly into the hold of the ship lying at anchor.

Tom Rule /10

Tom Rule was one of the best known of the Santa Ana pioneers. Tall and powerfully built, he was a Civil War veteran in his thirties when he went to work for the McFaddens at Newport Landing in 1875, shortly after the first arrival of the *Newport*. For a time he supervised the mud wharf warehouse in Wilmington, rented by James McFadden while he was carrying freight for Los Angeles merchants. After the sale of the *Newport*, Rule continued to occupy the building as it still contained property belonging to the McFaddens. One day Phineas T. Banning's agent, a Captain Browning, locked him out of the warehouse. Rule returned to Newport Landing where he awakened James McMillan, the pilot, by handing him a pistol and a box of cartridges and demanding his help in recapturing the mud wharf warehouse. He explained to McMillan that the gun was probably not necessary, "but it was often well to have one on exhibition."[1]

Newport Landing was the pioneer seaport for Santa Ana and surrounding farmlands. House in the foreground was the residence of Robert McFadden until 1884 when it became the pilot's home. The buildings at the water's edge are warehouses. Horse and mule-drawn wagons transported grain to the landing and carried lumber to inland areas. Sketch represents a view looking east across the mouth of the upper bay.

At Wilmington the two men approached the warehouse stealthily in a small boat. McMillan guarded the warehouse door while Rule entered the office and engaged Captain Browning in conversation, all the while pushing him backwards through the building and finally out the door. As soon as he had the agent outside, Rule placed himself in the doorway and said, "I take possession of the wharf and warehouse in the name of Captain McFadden! You can't come in here again, sir." Tom Rule remained in possession, but took a day off the following month to hear Denis Kearney, the San Francisco sandlot orator, who was to speak in Santa Ana. Kearney, campaigning on behalf of the Workingmen's Party, had gone all over California delivering eloquent speeches in his appealing Irish brogue. These orations were aimed at California's Chinese population, the railroad, large landowners, capitalists, and the "thieving scoundrelly rich." A contemporary described his methods of winning followers: "He arrives at a country town . . . picks up all the floating scandals about respectable citizens, which he incorporates into his tirade as absolute truth. This is done without investigation and with utter recklessness, and his falsehoods are seasoned with vulgar abuse and profanity."

The Workingmen's Party had won many sympathizers

who wanted to hear Kearney's talk. Even those who disagreed with his style and methods admired the Irishman's stand against the hated Southern Pacific Railroad and its leaders. And the speech was certain to provide entertainment. Wagons converged on Santa Ana's ungraded streets as men, women, and children arrived from the surrounding countryside to hear the famous sandlot orator. At four o'clock in the afternoon on March 19, 1879, Denis Kearney mounted a platform in front of the two-story frame hotel. Across the street the McFadden brothers stood in the doorway of a small wooden building that served as their office. With them was Tom Rule, their loyal but impetuous employee, "a splendid specimen of physical manhood and extraordinary strength."

Kearney began. First he advised squatters on disputed rancho lands to arm themselves with guns so they would not be evicted. Next he took out a piece of paper upon which he had written the names of local people who were "fit subjects for plunder and revenge." The name of James McFadden headed the list. Kearney claimed that McFadden had collected money from the people to buy a steamer, "and then when he couldn't get any more he sold out his steamer to the railroad company." McFadden stepped forward, climbed onto a buggy wheel where he could be seen, and asked for an explanation. Kearney turned to him and said, "You can't break up this meeting. No hell-born villain like you can break up this meeting!" McFadden pressed the matter no more, while Kearney proceeded with his list. He read the names of James Irvine, William Spurgeon, and realtor J. H. Fruit, making defamatory remarks about each.

After the meeting Kearney ate dinner at the hotel. When he came out, James McFadden and others asked him who had furnished his local information. One man pointed out that Santa Ana citizens had sent a fine carriage to Anaheim to carry him to the meeting in style, and had built a platform for his address. Why, then, had he abused them? Kearney answered, "I am a public agitator, and in that capacity I know no friends. I pick up local grievances and then ventilate them, and if anybody is hurt I can't help it." Bystanders saw that "Bob" McFadden was about to strike Kearney. Tom Rule stepped forward. He gave the sandlot orator a powerful blow on the face. Kearney ran into the hotel dining room for his pistol, which he had forgotten. The weapon was taken from him before he could use it. Rule chased him into the drug store and gave him a thorough beating from which he was rescued only by the arrival of Deputy Sheriff Hickey. Kearney was "one mass of blood and his head and face were swollen and terribly bruised." Wrapped in bandages, he climbed aboard the next stagecoach for San Diego.[2]

Newspaper headlines all over California announced the beating of Denis Kearney by Tom Rule. Editors praised and condemned Rule for weeks, but no one in Santa Ana ever thought he should be arrested. He was a hero, Some of his friends even suggested that he should run for president of the United States. Tom, "somewhat bored, wore his honors with becoming modesty."[3] Eventually he settled down with his wife and two children in a small house at Newport Landing. A year or so after the Kearney-Rule episode, the McFadden brothers built their three-level warehouse on the Irvine-owned bluff above the landing. Sacks of grain were brought by farmers to the upper level, stored in the middle section, and carried from the lower floor by a long hinged chute leading into the hold of the *Newport* anchored in the bay below. The landing was a busy place in the 1880s, as farmers arrived with grain and left with purchases of lumber and other building materials. Many pioneers remembered Tom Rule's feats of strength, demonstrated as he loaded and unloaded farm and lumber wagons.

Robert McFadden and his family lived in the largest house at the landing, a two-story redwood dwelling, until they moved to Santa Ana in 1884. After that the house was occupied by the pilot, and also served as a boarding house for employees. Longtime residents of the landing included the McMillan, Duarte, and Ortega families, Joe Barraca ("Indian Joe"), an Italian fisherman, Frank, and the old Portuguese shark fisherman, Manuel. James McMillan recalled that drinking water for the landing came from the old spring near the head of the upper bay. A rowboat, built especially for the purpose, was towed up the bay and filled by a V-shaped wooden trough. Because the water flowed so slowly, the boat was not towed back until the following day. Eventually Edward J. Abbott (no relation to Captain Dunnells' partner, William A. Abbott) settled on the peninsula across the bay, near today's Balboa pavilion. At *Abbott's Landing* he built a shack of timber cast adrift from lumber cargoes, and dug shallow wells that were a welcome source of water for campers. Abbott sent polished abalone shells to market by way of Newport Landing. The first trees on the peninsula were those in a cypress grove he planted. According to James McMillan, the peninsula was often covered with sea lions in the early years.

While life ashore was peaceful, navigation on the bay presented countless problems to the McFaddens and their pilots. The entrance was always dangerous. The channel shifted frequently and had to be sounded and marked every time the *Newport* was due. Sunken rocks near the entrance made sharp turns necessary. The *Coast Pilot* advised, "It is impracticable to make the sharp turn without letting go an anchor and allowing the steamer to straighten out against the flood tide."[4] According to Robert McFadden, the *Newport* sometimes came down so hard on the bar that "she would make a man's teeth rattle." Once she went aground on the sunken rocks and "when the tide went out her nose was way down, and the propeller was out of water." There were many near-accidents with the lighters.

When the long monopoly of the Southern Pacific was broken by the arrival of the Santa Fe, Southern California's boom of the 1880s was touched off. Demand for lumber and merchandise increased greatly in Santa Ana, Orange, Tustin, and other communities. The McFaddens, limited to cargoes brought every two weeks by the *Newport* and to lumber unloaded from an occasional schooner, could not share in the flourishing business being enjoyed by other ports. James McFadden's political influence finally won a congressional appropriation for a government survey of Newport Bay in 1887 to determine the feasibility of a federally financed project to build jetties and dredge channels. McFadden hoped that the bay would at least become a harbor of refuge, if not a real seaport that might challenge his old rival, San Pedro.

The 1887 survey was off to a bad start when fog forced Major W. H. H. Benyuard of the Army Corps of Engineers and a party of men to spend the night in a rowboat outside the Newport Bay entrance. After several weeks of investigation the army engineers announced that the necessary work at Newport, including the construction of twin rock

Tom Rule

Newport Landing site, late 1930s. The main part of the landing was on the beach; warehouse and chute were on the bluff.

knew of the unusually deep and quiet water at this location, having had it called to their attention by Indian Joe who showed them that the breakers were nearly always small at that point. Westdahl suggested that it would be an ideal location for an ocean shipping wharf, over which the largest commercial vessels might load and unload cargoes.

Before they had time to move their shipping business from inside the bay across to the peninsula beach, one last tragedy struck the proprietors of Newport Landing. On a July afternoon in 1887 Tom Rule and a youth named Miguel Ortega were rowing toward the bay entrance to mark the channel for the next arrival of the *Newport*. It was against the McFaddens' rules to sound the bar when the tide was going out, but reckless and fearless Tom Rule disobeyed the regulation. A great wave caught the rowboat and capsized it. Ortega swam ashore but Tom Rule drowned, injured when struck on the head by the tossing boat. All Santa Ana mourned. For the McFaddens, who had never forgotten Captain Pierce and the others, it was a heartbreaking incident.

By the end of 1888 the great wharf (at the site of today's Newport Beach municipal pier) was completed. It stood 19 feet above high water, 1300 feet long, and 60 feet wide at the outer end. A wooden bridge "across the Santa Ana River" at the west end of the lower bay now connected the peninsula with the mainland. Several houses and other buildings had been floated across the bay from the old landing to the new "outside landing." In December, 1888, the faithful *Newport* made her last trip in and out of the bay. She continued to call at California ports until 1892 when she became a whaling vessel and "went further north in Alaskan waters than did any other whaler of her time."[5]

jetties, would cost $1,500,000, an expense not justified because so little commerce had developed. To the McFaddens it seemed an outrageous verdict. How could commerce develop when ships could not enter? James McFadden was further angered when Congress made generous appropriations for harbor reclamation projects at San Pedro and Wilmington.

Superintendent George Davidson of the U.S. Coast Survey was sympathetic with the plight of the McFaddens. He directed his assistant, Ferdinand Westdahl, "to make a special examination of the physical hydrography off the beach west of the Newport Bay entrance, where one of the great submarine valleys heads." The McFaddens

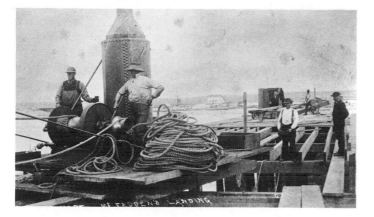

Building McFaddens' ocean wharf in the autumn of 1888. House on the beach was the former McFadden dwelling, floated across the bay from the landing.

Wharf construction crew, 1888.

Tom Rule

THE NEW OCEAN WHARF, stretching a quarter of a mile out into the ocean from the peninsula beach, dominated the tiny new community of tents and wooden buildings. William Schirmer, former officer on the *Newport* and pilot at the old landing, was the wharfinger in charge of the entire shipping enterprise. On the afternoon of January 9, 1889 he awaited two events: the birth of a child and the arrival of a ship. A few minutes after Mrs. Schirmer gave birth to a son, the Pacific Coast Steamship Company's 689-ton *Eureka* steamed up to the pier. The boy was named William Eureka Schirmer. The most colorful period in Newport's pioneer history began.

In his journal James McFadden recorded the *Eureka's* arrival, her unloading of ten tons of freight, and departure two hours later. On January 12 the *Bonita* left with 997 sheep. Two days later the *Los Angeles* discharged a cargo valued at $52.58. In his firm and legible handwriting McFadden noted on January 24 that the approach to the wharf was "made so teams can drive on it."[1] In February, according to the journal, McFadden went to Sacramento.

Three-masted vessel unloading at McFaddens' wharf in the 1890s.

Assemblyman E. E. Edwards of Santa Ana had introduced a bill in the California legislature to enable the southern forty miles of Los Angeles County to secede and form a new county. James McFadden, who blamed politics for his failures to obtain appropriations for Newport Harbor improvements, was a leader in the movement.

A. J. McFadden has described the trip made to Sacramento by James McFadden (his uncle) and William Spurgeon. "After they'd been up there about a week, they sent a telegram down to Santa Ana to send them ten thousand dollars. They needed the money to hire an attorney. He was an attorney all right, but as you can readily surmise, as a result of that selection, they got all of San Francisco's votes in favor of causing Los Angeles County to be divided."[2] The bill passed on March 11, 1889. Newly formed Orange County opened for business on August first. With a population of about 13,000, it was proud of its seaport at McFaddens' Wharf and its county seat at Santa Ana.

With an improved wagon road from Santa Ana to the beach, and a new bridge to the peninsula, hundreds of people enjoyed oceanside camping and picnicking for the first time in their lives. The second summer brought sadness with the tragic drowning of Lottie Spurgeon, sixteen year-old daughter of Santa Ana's founder. Young

Mrs. Sarah Salter, standing on the front porch of her store. She prescribed medicines, removed slivers and fishhooks, and even set broken bones. The nearest doctor was in Santa Ana.

Ocean front scene, west of the wharf, about 1895. The large building on the left is McFaddens' Hotel; the one on the right is Sharps Hotel.

people could talk of nothing else for weeks, but they learned the mysteries of rip tides and how to deal with them at Newport, where there would be no life guards for many years.

In 1890 the McFaddens built a railroad from the beach to Santa Ana. Rails, ties, and engine were brought by ship. The Santa Ana and Newport Railroad, with Edwin Smiley as its agent, began regular morning and evening runs in February, 1891. Connections were made with the Santa Fe in Santa Ana. To the astonishment and consternation of inland beach lovers, the trains never ran on Sunday. This meant that visitors — most of whom worked long six-day weeks — had to go by horse and wagon

if they wanted a Sunday outing at the beach. James McFadden, a founder of the Santa Ana Presbyterian Church and a lifelong elder, as his father had been, gave religious scruples as the reason for the Sunday ban. Contrary to popular legend, passenger tickets on the railroad were never free.

In 1892 McFadden received title to more than half the peninsula, including the wharf site, as "swamp and over-flow land" for which he paid the state of California a dollar an acre. In that year he had a townsite platted, leased lots at from $12 to $18 a year to those wishing to build cottages, and constructed the large oceanfront hotel that was a landmark for the next thirty years.

McFaddens' wharf was a quarter of a mile long, sixty feet wide at the outer end, and nineteen feet above the water at high tide. Fishermen and strollers enjoyed it on Sundays when "not a wheel turned on the railroad."

Sidewalks at Newport were two parallel planks across the sand. Permanent residents as well as campers carried drinking water in buckets from a large tank next to the wharf. Horse and mule-drawn vehicles were banished from the beach when McFadden constructed a feed yard which served as the local "parking lot" for many years.

Among the sandspit pioneers were the Schirmers mentioned earlier, the Duartes and others who had moved from the old landing, and the Salter and Sharps families. Late in 1892 the Sharps family moved its boom-time hotel from Capistrano Beach to Newport, to serve as a boarding house for McFadden employees. Jonathan Sharps was in charge of the town's water supply and railroad tank car. Mrs. Sharps, famous for her fish dinners, ran the hotel. Her father, Horace Salter, managed the feed yard, Mrs. Salter opened a small confectionary and curio store next door to Sharps Hotel. She was also the town's nurse and midwife. Other pioneer families of the 1890s were the B700cketts, Starcks, Struckenbrucks, Peabodys, Dixons, Hemstreets, Hawleys, and John McMillans. Life on the sandspit was primitive. Most of these first residents were poor people who helped one another when hardships arose. They lived largely on fish, clams, and abalones — supplemented now and then by wild ducks and geese. Life was also simple for visitors and summer residents who bathed in the surf, fished from the wharf,

Locomotive on the Santa Ana-Newport railroad. Large tank that supplied drinking water is shown at right.

Newport corral, looking across the future Lido Isle towards the upper bay.

and rowed up and down the bay.

Although a Mr. Grouard was said to have had a small steam launch on Newport Bay as early as 1887, the first such craft of record was Edward J. Abbott's *Last Chance*. The Los Angeles *Times* noted on May 24, 1892: "The *Last Chance* was built on Newport Bay . . . and is launched for the purpose of giving excursions on the bay. During the summer months moonlight excursions to the beach are quite popular, and now that an enjoyable ride over the bay may be added to the evening of pleasure, moonlight parties during the coming season will probably be all the rage, especially with the young people of the county." The *Times* announced the following week that Abbott had received his certificate of "hull and boiler"

inspection and that "the *Last Chance* will make a run of about twelve miles on the bay and will be finished for the accommodation of pleasure parties."[3] According to H. L. Sherman, however, Abbott was never granted a license to run the boat on Newport Bay. Two years later the *Last Chance* went to Lake Elsinore via horse-drawn wagon and Santa Fe freight car.[4]

In the middle 1890s the V. V. Tubbs and C. F. Bennett families of Tustin, along with the E. E. Keech family of Santa Ana, vacationed in simple wooden summer houses built next to Abbott's Landing. They called the place Bayside. Today it is Balboa. These three families and their friends owned a fleet of about seven sailboats. All were home-made except Attorney E. E. Keech's

There were no lifeguards in the early days, but a lifeline through
the breakers offered security to bathers, many of whom could not swim.

Vacationing at Newport. Summer cottages stood on stilts,
a safe distance above rising ocean or bay waters.

"round bottomed, professionally built" boat. Mr. Keech
won all the races, but his sailboat was so tippy that it
capsized nearly every time he took it out on the bay.
Mrs. Keech, mother of five, spent most of her time over
a washtub until her husband filled burlap bags with the
laundry and tied them around the outside of the boat.
Dragging through the water, they stabilized the craft.
The family would cruise around all afternoon. When
evening came they would wring out the clothes and
spread them on the sand dunes to dry. But few people
sought the solitude of the peninsula in the 1890s. Most
came to Newport to bathe in the surf or fish from the
pier.

Everything else at Newport was dwarfed by the great
railroad pier. It was the heart of the community. Ships
tied up, sometimes as many as three at a time, while
others lay at anchor waiting to unload. The railroad station stood on the inner end of the wharf. Everyone in
town went to meet the morning and evening trains.
Catches of fish were enormous. The men who fished
for a living rowed dories to sea early in the morning
and rigged sails to take advantage of the breezes as they
returned. It was during the 1890s that the custom arose
of having the dorymen's wives sell the freshly caught
fish each day. The first booths were beneath the wharf.
Later the women began to use the boats as shops. Crowds
came to watch the seining, when teams of horses drew
nets bulging with smelt ashore through the surf.

Newport was a regular port of call for the old 521-ton wooden steamer *Bonita*, a "hog boat" that carried cattle, sheep, hogs, and poultry from Orange County.

V. V. Tubbs at the tiller of his tippy sailboat, one of the earliest pleasure craft on Newport Bay.

John A. Campbell, 546 tons, was one of many large sailing vessels that brought lumber to Newport in the late 1890s.

The schooner *Excelsior*, with a load of lumber for
Orange County.

The *John A. Campbell* at McFaddens' Wharf.

Meeting the *Corona*, a familiar sight at Newport
in the 1890s.

The 2415-ton iron steamer *Santa Rosa* brought freight
and passengers.

The McFadden railroad and wharf, with a payroll of a hundred men, was the largest business Orange County had ever known. Grain, meat, eggs, citrus fruit, and farm animals were shipped as more and more of the county's fertile land was cultivated. When James Irvine II, a young man still in his twenties, began to develop the agricultural potential of the San Joaquin Ranch, his barley, beans, and sugar beets rolled to the wharf by the carload. Ships put in from Washington, Oregon, and California ports. Many were steamers, but great numbers of three- and four-masted lumber schooners also called. Sailing ships that tied up at McFadden's wharf included *Fred E. Sander, Halcyon, John A. Campbell, Emma Claudina, Challenger, Reporter, Albert Meyer, American Girl, Lottie Carson, Mary E. Russ, Maria E. Smith, Centralia, J. M. Griffith, Excelsior,* and *Louise.* Among the steamers were *Eureka, Corona, Pomona, Coos Bay, Farallon, South Coast, Navarro, Caspar, Newberg, Tillamook, Rival, Westport, Noyo, Santa Cruz, Queen of the Pacific, Los Angeles, Santa Rosa, Bonita, St. Paul, Mexico, Jewel,* and *Homer.*

Sailing without radio, radar, or other modern navigational aids, few vessels lasted long enough at that time to be scrapped when their useful days were over. Among the steamers that put in at the Newport wharf, the *St. Paul* piled up on the rocks off Point Joe, Monterey Peninsula, in 1896. In 1908 the *Pomona* struck an uncharted rock off Fort Ross and sank. During a violent snowstorm in 1910 the *Farallon* went to pieces on rocks in Alaskan waters. The *Santa Rosa* broke up in a dense fog north of Point Arguello in 1911. The *Coos Bay* was destroyed by mountainous seas at Ventura in 1914. In 1924 fire destroyed the *Santa Cruz.*

Although his ocean shipping business was successful, James McFadden continued to hope for federally-financed harbor reclamation. It was perhaps with this in mind that he bought the two large marshes (later filled to become Lido and Balboa Islands) as swamp and overflow land in 1896. In the following year he built an eleven-mile spur to his railroad, extending it northwest to the flourishing celery fields of Smeltzer. In spite of this expansion, McFadden suddenly sold his wharf, railroad, and the Smeltzer line in 1899.

Throughout the decade a "free harbor" fight had been waged in Congress. Southern Pacific Railroad interests wanted a Los Angeles harbor at Santa Monica that they could control exclusively. Los Angeles citizens, led by Senator Stephen White, demanded a publicly owned harbor at San Pedro. They won the fight in April, 1899, along with a federal appropriation of almost three million dollars for harbor improvements. No ocean wharf at Newport could compete with a safe, deep, sheltered harbor as near as San Pedro. When Colonel William Holabird, a promoter, approached James McFadden and offered to buy his railroad for J. Ross Clark and W. A. Clark, who (he said) wanted to extend the Smeltzer line to their sugar factory at Los Alamitos, McFadden accepted. The price was $400,000. Two months later, in June, 1899, the railroad was turned over to his old enemy, the Southern Pacific. It appeared that the railroad had been the undisclosed purchaser and that McFadden had been tricked, but it is doubtful that all the details of this transaction will ever be known.

Excursionists welcomed the Sunday trains put on the Newport railroad by the Southern Pacific as soon as it took control, but many loyal friends of the McFaddens

James Irvine II (1867-1947) once rode from San Francisco to the San Joaquin ranch on this venerable ancestor of today's ten-speed models. Unlike his father, who had used the ranch mainly for sheep, young James was to devote his life to developing its agricultural potential. In the 1890s large cargoes of barley and other products from the San Joaquin ranch were sent to northern cities via the McFaddens' railway and wharf.

refused to ship farm products through Newport. James Irvine sent his barley to San Diego by the Santa Fe Railroad, to be loaded on ships bound for San Francisco. Eventually the Southern Pacific made freight rates to Newport the same as those to San Pedro, thus killing the shipping business at McFaddens' Wharf. The great ships ceased to put in. Newport's glorious decade as an ocean shipping port was over. In the spring of 1902, three years after his sale of the railroad and wharf, McFadden sold his remaining Newport Bay holdings, about 840 acres, to William S. Collins and A. C. Hanson, for a price said to have been between $35,000 to $50,000. Included were the townsite and hotel, half the Newport-Balboa peninsula, swamplands at the west end of the bay, and the marshes that are now Harbor, Lido, and Balboa Islands. In the transfer of these areas to Collins and Hanson, a technical flaw appeared in the title. McFadden had bought "swamp and overflow land," leaving a question as to whether he owned just the areas above the high tide line or the tidelands (areas between the daily rise and fall of the tides) as well. James McFadden's friend, Senator George C. Perkins, president of the Pacific Coast Steamship Company introduced a bill into Congress. The measure, signed by the President, perfected Collins' and Hanson's title to the tidelands.

For James McFadden it was the end of more than thirty years as the leading Newport Bay pioneer. But his hopes of an improved harbor, dating back to his first visit in 1868, had never been realized. A few years later, at the age of 82, he said, "Newport Harbor was once a hobby with me, but my efforts there were not a success. Besides, the loss of several friends has been a grief."[5]

A New Century /12

A<small>T</small> <small>THE</small> <small>TURN</small> of the century, as Victorian days came to an end, a Los Angeles newspaper noted: "Not more than two or three of the ten people who bathe in the sea can swim at all, and probably not one in ten can swim any considerable distance." But times were changing. With increasing leisure, people were becoming interested in water sports. "The art of diving and the pretty effects, where it is done gracefully, have come to be quite an attraction at the watering places. . . . Boating has been the subject of increasing attention of late. The correct handling of oars has been a matter of special study, and the adjustment of sheet and tiller has developed interestingly in numerous sailing races."[1]

Los Angeles, with a population of 102,000 people in 1900, began reaching out to beach and resort areas. Henry E. Huntington, nephew of Collis P. Huntington of the Southern Pacific, had bought the Sherman-Clark electric railway system in Los Angeles and initiated its expansion all over Southern California. The swift, efficient Red Cars would eventually bind farmlands, beaches, and moun-

tains into a community that is the foundation of today's metropolitan Los Angeles.

The McFadden settlement of Newport had become almost a ghost town since the sale of the wharf and railroad, and termination of the once-lively shipping business. When W. S. Collins and A. C. Hanson took over the site in 1902 they announced that town lots, previously leased by the year, must be purchased by June 1 for $125 or more. This came as a blow to the fishermen and wharf workers (paid $2.00 a day during the 1890s), many of whom had never paid ground rent but lived as squatters on the least desirable lots during the previous decade. The new owners did not, however, press the matter. Many old timers, including Indian Joe and Sam Plestini, a Slavonic fisherman, remained in their shacks on the bayfront while Collins and Hanson began to "clean up the premises" of what was now advertised as the "Queen of the Beaches."

Handsome, debonair William S. Collins, co-purchaser of James McFadden's sandy and marshy Newport holdings, was a promoter. Still in his thirties, he owned interests in an automobile factory, Arizona mines, oil wells, a loan company, and the boom-time hotel at Fairview (north Costa Mesa). A biographical history published at this time describes him as a man with "wonderful powers

The Balboa pavilion, Newport Bay's most famous landmark, as it looked in 1911. Hotel Balboa, right, was built in ten days, in time for arrival of the first Red Car on July 4, 1906.

of application and concentration," the type of man who "understands the manipulation of money and brains, who has the supreme organization and management, and who can lead many minds, however diverse, into one resistless current of progress and enlightenment . . ."[2]

Collins soon dropped Hanson as his associate and took on none other than Henry E. Huntington himself as one of the partners in his Newport Beach Company. The Red Car magnate, in exchange for a part of the inner end of the peninsula and "Huntington" (Lido) Island, gave Collins $37,500 and a promise to extend the Pacific Electric to Newport.

Suddenly the boom was on. It seemed as if Southern California had just discovered the beach towns. Prices sky-rocketed at Santa Monica, Redondo, Long Beach, Sunset Beach, and Huntington Beach (formerly Pacific City). The greatest sensation was Abbott Kinney's new town of Venice with its canals, breakwater, pavilion, bath house, aquarium, roller coaster, and auditorium with an immense pipe organ. Newport could not aspire to anything so grand, but Collins laid a few water pipes and boardwalks while losing and gaining more partners. Lots jumped from $125 to $250 and up.

By 1905 several new subdivisions had sprung up around Newport Bay, all impatiently waiting for the first Pacific Electric train to bring crowds of buyers. But the rails seemed to creep at a snail's pace from Huntington Beach. There were excuses. "Too many trestles to build," or "wire must be ordered from the East." But on June 3, 1905 the Santa Ana *Blade* stated that the electric road was "now being pushed as fast as several hundred men and an army of scrapers, shovels, plows, and teams can grade

the road and lay the track, with all the energy and spirit that the Huntington road builders are known to possess." On August 3, 1905, the first Red Car reached Newport, bringing the railroad's dignitaries, including Henry E. Huntington who was taken for a ride on the bay. Three days later the first crowds of passengers arrived, following a ride from Los Angeles that had taken little more than an hour. Ready to meet them were agents from all the tracts — ready with the Santa Ana band, horses and buggies, gasoline launches, and free lunches. Visitors boarded boats to East Newport, Balboa, Corona del Mar, and even the future Balboa Island, where nearly all the lots were under water.

Collins had by now sold the original Newport townsite to Stephen Townsend who refurbished the two old hotels (Sharps' and McFadden's) and built a small, square, open-air pavilion on the ocean front. Townsend also had interests in the "canal" tract and a children's bathing pool being dredged at West Newport. Eastward along the peninsula, the building that is now the Newport Harbor Yacht Club was being built on a watery site belonging to the East Newport Town Company, headed by W. W. Wilson of Riverside. Planks led from the marshy shore to Bay Island, the only island high and dry enough in the beginning not to require dredging, though it was later enlarged. Here R. J. Waters and Rufus Sanborn of Tustin, having paid $350 for the island and a barn location on the peninsula, were organizing the "Bay Island Club."

Next came Abbott's Landing, and Bayside, where the new Balboa tract was being developed. Here J. P. Greeley, F. W. Harding, and other shareholders in the Newport Bay Investment Company were laying out a summer colony on land bought from Joseph Ferguson. Barges brought dirt for surfacing the streets, and lumber for building the picturesque pavilion that is still Newport Bay's most famous landmark. The name "Balboa" was selected by E. J. Louis, one of its developers, who visualized a huge figure of Balboa standing with one foot on Catalina and the other on the Newport peninsula. Beyond Balboa, the only building was a small house belonging to Joseph Ferguson, owner of the peninsula point. By this time W. S. Collins was established at Balboa where he had opened a machine shop and Collins Commercial Company. Here he was building a dredger. Out in the bay lay his last unsold Newport holding, a marsh that had been called Snipe Island, Crusoe Island, and Newport Island (a name later given by Ralph Maskey to an island in the canal tract). Eventually it would become Balboa Island, Collins' lasting claim to fame.

From Balboa the launch *Flora* took passengers to George Hart's subdivision above Rocky Point, now Corona del Mar. Here even James Irvine had decided to sell some land in the ever-spiraling boom. Drought years had been hard on his already-mortgaged ranch, and Irvine welcomed the opportunity to sell 700 "non-productive" acres at the inflated price of $150 an acre. Corona del Mar was a desolate, isolated place, reached overland only by a long, muddy road around the upper bay. Hart was erecting a water tank on the hill and planning to build a hotel.

A number of cottages were built in 1905, mostly little one-story brown bungalows trimmed with white. On Bay Island, where a windmill was erected, houses were in the "pagoda style." But as winter came it was evident that Newport, at the end of the Pacific Electric line, could

The Red Cars of the Pacific Electric reached Newport Beach in 1905 and Balboa in 1906. A ride to downtown Los Angeles took about an hour.

expect no boom such as that enjoyed by Redondo and other places closer to Los Angeles. No one knew whether the Red Cars would ever reach Balboa but some hoped they would go even farther — right across the mouth of the bay! It was at the end of this year that Dr. Albert Soiland, later Southern California's leading yachtsman,

59

Newport Bay, looking east from below present site of Hoag Hospital, showing Southern Pacific trestle and bridge for wagons and automobiles. About 1910.

John Scarpa and his gondola on Newport Bay, 1909.

visited Newport Bay with a friend, Dr. Frank Miller. Years later he described the trip from Los Angeles on a drizzly winter day:

> After riding for an hour or more, the last part of which was along the old Pacific, we arrived at the little fishing village of Newport, the line's terminus, and although the rain was increasing, our spirits had been revived by the fresh air.
>
> It was peaceful. To the southeast stretched a long, sandy beach, hardened by the rain, along which we were soon briskly walking. After about a mile, the rain became serious and we sought shelter. We spied a little clump of scrubby pine trees a little further down and, nearby, a single cottage with lazy smoke oozing out of its brick chimney. It seemed like an oasis in the desert so we hastened and made bold to knock on the door. A friendly appearing man opened up, bade us welcome, and brought chairs up to the cheery fireplace. With our outer clothing removed, we were soon snug and warm. It developed that we were being entertained by Mr. Fred Strange who had just moved in from Riverside for the purpose of starting a new subdivision on this desert spot, for the East Newport Town Company, and that he would show us the maps. After another hot toddy graciously furnished by our genial host, we became deeply interested in the magnificent subdivision which Mr. Strange solemnly assured us was about to spring forth like the smoke from Aladdin's Lamp. Dr. Miller and myself soon selected two adjoining lots on the Bay Front and plunked down ten dollars each on the total purchase price of $1500.00 . . . .

When we asked about our lots, he pointed out through the swamp directly in front of us about two hundred yards and said, "there they are." But he hastily added that the Company was immediately starting a dredging campaign which would bring our lots out high and dry on the new bay front in short order. Reassured, we made ready to start for home, but our host insisted we should not walk to Old Newport. A ride on the Company's "yacht" was the thing. So he led the way to the Pavilion where we found one Sandy tinkering with a dinky one-horse gasoline motor on the sorriest looking and most decrepit flat-bottomed skiff imaginable. Sandy twisted the flywheel with all his might, and after a few snorts, coughs, and wheezes, the propeller began to turn and the craft started to wiggle out from under the Pavilion shed, bumping over the grass and weeds, and jerkily made its way through a tortuous channel for the open bay. Every now and then Sandy would get out the single oar and help the motor push us over a shallow spot. The rain was again making us miserable and we looked longingly toward the Newport shore so far away. Suddenly, without warning, something popped within the engine and we were all showered with muddy, sticky grease and hot water. Investigation showed that the cylinder head had cracked wide open, and on our faces and over our clothing we felt the impact of all the aforesaid accumulations of the old engine. There we were — no engine, one oar, right over the oyster beds, and in the middle of Newport Bay. Oh! for a pair of rubber boots or a raft. However, by dint of poking, with Sandy walk-

Helena Modjeska, the great Polish Shakespearean actress, bought this pagoda-style house at #3 Bay Island in 1908 and died there the following year. Modjeska was the first celebrity to become a year-round resident of Newport Beach. The house was replaced in 1941.

ing astern and pushing, we finally made Newport, wet and bedraggled, but fortunate in catching the last afternoon car for Los Angeles.[3]

Balboa, Cal., looking West, Bay Island in Distance.

Balboa Island /13

I<small>N THE SPRING OF</small> 1906 W. S. Collins' new dredger began creating a channel along the bay shore of East Newport and Balboa, and filling small tracts of land such as those bought the previous winter by Dr. Soiland and Dr. Miller. Developers of Corona del Mar, Balboa, and East Newport were overjoyed when news came that the Red Car line would be extended to the Balboa pavilion. Carpenters hastened to build a new fifteen-room Balboa Hotel. The arrival of the Pacific Electric on the Fourth of July was a wildly celebrated event. On August 21, 1906, the three small communities of Newport, East Newport, and Balboa voted to incorporate as the city of Newport Beach.

Civic leaders of the three neighborhoods agreed that Southern California's boom in beach real estate was over, and that year-round sources of income must be found. Their principal asset was undeveloped Newport Bay. Looking back to Newport's great era as a shipping port, they began to dream of a great commercial harbor. Sixteen men, calling themselves the "Harbor Boosters," met early in 1907 and established a chamber of commerce pledged to the creation of a deep, safe, navigable harbor. These men, who contributed five dollars each to a fund

Picture postcard view from the Balboa Pavilion toward Bay Island, about 1910.

for initial expenses, were W. W. Crosier, A. A. Lester, John King, George T. Peabody, C. L. Lancaster, C. S. Hemstreet, J. H. Sharps, C. A. Barton, Albert Hermes, L. S. Wilkinson, Joseph Ferguson, Lew H. Wallace, Terrel Jasper, John McMillan, W. W. Wilson, and Fred Beckwith. Nearly all were gone before the final reclamation was completed thirty years later, but many of them devoted years of their lives to the creation of Newport Harbor. Initially they persuaded Captain Amos A. Fries of the Army Corps of Engineers to inspect the bay. He admitted in 1907 that a good harbor might be developed at Newport, but gave the boosters no encouragement. "Where is your commerce?" he asked. This refrain was to echo in their ears for years to come: *"Where is your commerce?"* Without commerce the federal government could offer no help.

With the cooperation of James Irvine, plans were made for a future seaport at "Port Orange," at the site of old Newport Landing. A townsite was laid out on the bluffs above, in the hope that eventually it would overlook a great shipping center where "ships and rails will meet." Port Orange had a new sidewheel excursion boat, with a pilot who was an expert at avoiding mud flats and sandbars when he had prospective purchasers aboard. Irvine also sold several hundred acres to Stephen Townsend who opened the Newport Heights tract, some of which soon became the nucleus of Harper, later Costa Mesa.

Although his name does not appear on the list of Newport Harbor's sixteen original boosters, a young future booster visited Balboa on a Pacific Electric picnic excursion in the summer of 1907. He was Joseph A. Beek, a student at Pasadena's Throop Institute (later California Institute of Technology). Beek and his friends walked along the board walk toward the Balboa Pavilion, "new and resplendent with shining bright paint and flags." He recalled that "On Main Street there was the Balboa Hotel, a restaurant, a real estate office, the latter about six by twelve . . . A part of the street, as I remember it, had been surfaced from the electric line to the pavilion, while a plank walk led to the Balboa pier. I do not remember seeing any automobiles that day. There were some horses and buggies and quite a lot of people milling around."

Beek ate his lunch in the old Abbott cypress grove but did not remember what he ate because "I was feasting my eyes on what to me was the most intriguing prospect I had ever seen. Northward, across the sparkling blue waters of the bay there was a low sand island with two houses on it. To the east and north of the island I noted that the incoming tide was flooding a wide extent of sand bars and filling numerous little channels and lagoons. Most interesting of all was a winding channel which I could vaguely make out skirting the bluff on the north side of the bay. The island, of course, was what grew into Balboa Island. The channel referred to formed part of what we now [1936] call the north bay. A small steam dredge was working between Balboa Island and Harbor Island [then only a marsh]. There were half a dozen motor boats, and a number of row boats and canoes, but I do not recall any sail boats."[1]

Later that year John Scarpa, an Italian gondolier, grew weary of the canals at the California Venice where he never felt like singing. Scarpa "sculled his gondola from Playa del Rey to Newport Bay. Entering the harbor in those days, long before the first breakwater, was no feat for a weakling, but the stout-hearted Scarpa triumphantly guided his craft over and through the foaming billows to a haven on the placid waters beyond."[2] There he could sing once more as his gondola wound through the green marshlands of Newport Bay. "Many fashionable people of the day" enjoyed daytime and moonlight rides into the upper bay and "up the Santa Ana River." In the summer of 1908 Scarpa staged a Venetian illuminated night water parade, beginning an annual tradition that later became the Tournament of Lights. Scarpa's gondola led the way, followed by eight canoes, all lighted with Japanese lanterns. One of the canoeists was Fred Beckwith, manager of the Balboa pavilion and head of the local canoe club.

Early in 1909 W. S. Collins finished dredging the north side of Balboa Island and announced plans to do additional dredging on the south side. When he applied to the Orange County supervisors for permission to fill the large tideland area (to which he had good title as a result of Senator Perkins' efforts), local newspapers described it as the "Rape of Newport Harbor." Boosters complained that the remaining channel would be too narrow, tide prism would be reduced, scour would diminish, and the harbor would be permanently ruined. The Army Corps of Engineers sent Captain D. E. Hughes to look into the matter. In a letter to his superior, Hughes visualized a future time "when multitudes will seek Newport Bay for pleasure and rest."

"I wonder," he wrote in 1909, "how much we today should do towards conserving the God-given right of the pleasure of sailing hither and yon over these quiet land-locked waters that yet belong to all the people. Shall we acquiesce in having them narrowed down for the sole benefit of any individual who looks back at only the dollar per acre paid, and forward to only the hundreds of dollars a lot which he does not need?"[3] W. S. Collins, who was an affable man, abandoned his plans to enlarge the south side of his island. As teams of horses drawing fresno scrapers smoothed out the sand deposited on the island in great long ridges by the dredger, Collins began plans for a seawall. Balboa Island stood level with the high tide line, but this was not high enough. American cement was expensive. Knowing that vessels loading at San Pedro had often arrived empty from Europe, Collins arranged for German cement to be brought on return trips — all the way around Cape Horn. "He got the cement at low cost and the ships got the ballast." Much has been written about this famous original Balboa Island sea wall, built of cheap German cement and beach sand. For years island residents never knew when bay waters would come seeping into their living rooms.

A more sturdy structure than the wall was the Venetian mansion of reinforced concrete (of the same German cement) that Collins built for himself and his fourth wife, Apolena, on a small island, Collins Isle, at the west end of Balboa Island. Long known as "Collins' Castle," the two-story building was surrounded by pergolas and gardens. An arched entrance graced the boat landing, with steps leading to the water. The numerous downstair

rooms were filled with furniture popular in the period, but the upstairs was unlike anything else in pre-World War I Newport Beach. Above an elaborate, over-sized bed in the one large chamber a vast ceiling was painted with murals of nymphs and cherubs.

By 1910 the affluent were buying automobiles. Beach communities blamed "horseless carriages" for the poor sales of resort property. Who wanted a beach house ($500 and up) if he could buy a car instead? Collins, himself an automobile fancier, announced new plans for the development of Balboa Island. It was being laid out, he claimed, for the "automobile age." Previously he had planned a lagoon in the center, with Venetian canals radiating out to the bay. Now, instead, there would be an automobile speedway encircling the island, just inside the first row of houses. Collins also promised a six-car ferry and a large freight ferry, neither of which materialized although a small passenger launch, the *Teal*, had been put in service between the island and the peninsula in 1909. Joseph A. Beek has described the *Teal* and her black skipper, John Watts:

W. S. Collins built this Venetian-styled mansion for himself and his fourth wife, Apolena, on a small island at the west end of Balboa Island. Long known as Collins' Castle, the house was bought in the 1930s by actor James Cagney, who leased it to the Coast Guard during World War II.

Fortunately for John the mechanism of the ferry-boat Teal was not as complex as that of modern boats. The single cylinder engine was of the open crankcase type with a connecting rod plying back and forth in unblushing nakedness. The ignition was of the antiquated wipe-spark type while the modesty of the clutch knew not the shielding ministrations of a gear case.

John believed in the application of lots of oil, but seemed to pin more faith on gasoline as a cure-all for any ills his boat might develop. After cranking the engine, he used to seize a priming can and apply a little of its contents to everything in sight. The igniter came in for a dose, the reverse band on the clutch, the hub of the steering wheel and any other place that happened to arrest his attention. Fortunately the Teal was an open boat and there is no report of a fire or explosion.

John's ministrations to the engine required only an abstract attention on his part and never interfered perceptibly with the flow of conversation. If John was silent there was something wrong — but John was seldom silent.[4]

Mary Evalyn Rider, a summer vacationer, remembered John Watts as "the self-appointed guardian of all the younger generation who vacationed on the Island, much to our embarrassment at times, for he used to come sputtering across the bay at the most unheard of early hours of the evening, march into the dance hall, and literally drag us out. He'd say, "You all come out'a he'a now — it's ten o'clock.""[5]

In the summer of 1911 Collins ran a large advertisement for Balboa Island in the Los Angeles *Times* announcing that the government had granted a permit for the construction of "a mammoth concrete bridge to the island" and that Newport Bay would soon have a "mammoth breakwater and jetty." Lots on Balboa Island were $325 and up. At Balboa, where lots were $400 and up, the developers advertised "fishing, boating, canoeing, motoring, house parties, tennis, gondolas, hunting, cozy cottages, clam bakes, moonlight canoe rides, yacht parties, canoe carnivals, dining, surf fishing, croaker fishing, cockle and clam digging, cave exploration, attractive side trips, and horseback riding."

In spite of all these attractions, Newport Beach was scarcely a "fashionable watering place." Although a number of substantial bungalows had been built along the peninsula, there were only a few houses at Corona del Mar and about twenty cottages on Balboa Island. The official 1910 census showed a permanent population of only 445 persons. As 1911 opened there were complaints that the town was not being kept up. The boardwalk between East Newport and Balboa was warped and rickety, houses looked neglected, and paint was peeling. The hastily and cheaply installed electric, water, and sewer systems were undependable and a source of constant annoyance to residents. Newport realtors complained that fishermen's shanties at Newport, visible from the Pacific Electric tracks, created a bad impression. The fishermen pointed out that they were poorly paid for long and arduous hours of work, often receiving only two cents a pound for the fish. In addition, they had a special grievance in 1911 in which they were joined by nearly all temporary and permanent residents. The upper bay had been declared a game preserve.

66

Duck Hunting, Yachting, and Aviation /14

ORANGE COUNTY PIONEER Thomas B. Talbert has written: "This section of the country along the coast between Long Beach and Newport Beach, south of Westminster, was one of the greatest natural habitats for wild life and game birds in the world. Wild ducks, geese, jack-snipe, coots, plover, doves, killdeer, egrets, herons, gulls, pelicans, land birds, and waterfowl of every kind and description varied their flights from ocean to swamp, from swamp to grain fields, from grain fields to ocean again, to feast on seafood, grain, seeds, bugs, toads, worms, grasshoppers, and the like. I have seen birds by the thousands so thick in flight as to almost eclipse the sun. The hours-long flight of ducks patterned against a blazing sunset sky was most amazingly spectacular and beautiful. When startled, great flocks of birds arose to circle around and return to their beloved haven."[1]

In the early 1900s a number of shooting clubs bought land in Orange County and built club houses. Four were situated in the Newport Bay area, the most prestigious being the San Joaquin Gun Club, located northeast of the upper bay on land leased from James Irvine. Most of its members were wealthy Los Angeles men who sometimes shot more than the limit of 25 ducks a day and often did not bother to pick them up off the ground.

In 1910 M. J. Connell, head of the California Fish and Game Commission and a member of the San Joaquin Gun Club, arranged to have the Newport Upper Bay declared a game refuge, out of bounds for duck hunting. Under Connell's direction the game warden chased hunters away as he patrolled the upper bay in his boat, "beating" the birds toward the gun club. Local residents, who had lived off the land since pioneer days, were outraged, as were the hundreds of hunters who came from Los Angeles by Pacific Electric, sleeping on the beach all night to begin shooting at sunrise the next morning.

Editor Walter Cornelius of the Newport *News* took the lead in an attack against Connell and the San Joaquin Gun Club, charging: "Mr. Connell knew that upper Newport Bay was the resort of thousands of ducks and geese, and as the gun club is immediately adjoining, his fertile brain conceived the plan of prohibiting the public from hunting in the bay, and using it as a feeding ground for the gun club. The club built a dam across the east end of the bay, put several sink balls in it, and the members had absolutely the best shooting in Southern California as the ducks flew from the bay to the fresh water on the gun club . . . one of the wardens told the writer that he used to pick up ducks for the gun club on shooting days, and all the while he was drawing pay from the

Newport Beach banker Lew Wallace and two small
daughters, on horseback. Wallace, the leading Newport
Harbor "booster," used this method of transportation
between his home at East Newport and his bank near the wharf.

state."[2] The airing of the matter by the *Newport News*
resulted in the abolition of the upper bay game preserve
by Governor Hiram Johnson. But hunters had new complaints. Gasoline launches were frightening the birds
away.

Yachting as a sport took second place to duck hunting
in 1911, but Newport Bay already had about 25 or 30
motorboats, a few sailboats, and two hundred rowboats
and canoes. To most people, life on the water was a way
of earning a living, and a dangerous one at that. There
was a romance about the ocean, but "yachting" brought

to mind names like Commodore Vanderbilt and Sir
Thomas Lipton. When the average man became interested
in boating early in the twentieth century, he wanted a
new-fangled naphtha or gasoline launch. Dr. Albert
Soiland's first boat, *Viking I*, an "eighteen-foot open run-
about with a one-cylinder Ferro motor," was built in
his Hollywood back yard and sent to Newport Bay by
horse and wagon.

By 1911 Thomas Fleming Day, editor of the *Rudder*
magazine, was doing all he could to build up confidence
in the new sport of yachting. Having crossed the Atlantic
in the summer of 1911 in a 25-foot yawl, Day repeated
the exploit the following summer in a small motor cruiser.
These voyages must have been noticed in Los Angeles
where Dr. Soiland and a group of friends had organized
the South Coast Yacht Club, with headquarters at San
Pedro. Soiland's *Viking II*, a 35-foot motor cruiser, had
been constructed in his back yard and taken to San Pedro
by Pacific Electric flat car in 1909. Attempts to take the
vessel in and out of the Newport Bay entrance nearly
cost the doctor his life and his boat. At his wife's insis-
tance he promised not to try again until a jetty had been
built.

At Easter time in 1911 South Coast Yacht Club members
and their wives went to East Newport from Los Angeles
via Pacific Electric, stayed in cottages overnight, admired
the bay (at high tide), and danced at the Balboa pavilion.
Delighted with what they found, the yachtsmen arranged
to rent the East Newport pavilion (since 1919 the permanent home of the Newport Harbor Yacht Club) as Station
"A" of the South Coast Yacht Club. Shortly afterward
all the motorboats on Newport Bay, including those used
commercially, joined the new club. The Los Angeles

members did not move their boats to Newport, but cruised down the coast occasionally from San Pedro and anchored in the ocean, offshore of the wharf where "good old Joe Dixon would go out in his dory and land the gang through the surf. Many times he capsized, and the wet and bedraggled sailors would come down to the dance to dry out before the big fireplace in the pavilion. Those were the days of iron men and wooden ships."[3]

From the beginning, Los Angeles yachtsmen did all they could to encourage Newport's "Harbor Boosters" to work for jetties and other needed improvements. The need of establishing pier and bulkhead lines had been of concern ever since Collins' attempt two years earlier to increase the size of Balboa Island, but nothing had been done. In 1911, boosters and yachtsmen raised $300 to send Lew Wallace, the local banker and leading harbor booster, to Washington. Wallace, a native of North Dakota "who became seasick, even in a rowboat," was never an avid yachtsman but for many years he headed all attempts to create a navigable harbor. His mission in 1911 was to obtain a congressional appropriation for a survey of the bay and the establishment of harbor lines. He came home triumphant, with assurances of a federal grant of $2500 for that purpose. Because travel expenses had been only $267, he returned $33 to the donors. The survey was to take place the following summer.

Grateful citizens believed that "Before long we shall see the masts of sailing vessels and the smokestacks of steamers in the harbor of Newport Beach."[4] W. S. Collins, the perennial optimist, announced that he would build a two-story, 150-room hotel with a roof garden — on Balboa Island. He had not yet built the promised "mammoth concrete bridge" from Balboa Island to the mainland, but he hired young Joe Beek to help build a wooden one. Beek recalled that he furnished his own tools, bought on credit, and waited several days for building materials to arrive on the *Airplane*, "a black barge with a motor in it. It had a ramp on the forward end which could be lowered to the beach. This landing barge was used to transport lumber, cement, sewer tile, and other material to the shores of Balboa Island from whence it was distributed by team and wagon, there being no surfaced roads on Balboa Island in those days."[5] The 12-foot-wide bridge built in the summer of 1912 was crooked, uneven, and unbeautiful," but it lasted twelve years. At first only one team and wagon crossed it as there was no bridge across the upper bay and almost no other traffic from the mainland. Although automobiles made their way along the narrow road down the peninsula, most visitors still came by Pacific Electric or Southern Pacific.

In May, 1912, a crowd of people arrived by Red Car, rented rooms at the Balboa Hotel, and emerged in costume. The women wore old-fashioned peasant dresses, the men knee breeches or fishing costumes consisting of "oil skins, sou'westers, and fringes of whiskers around their necks." Loading themselves and a few portable houses into boats, they crossed to Corona del Mar where they borrowed two cows from the Irvine Company, set up camera equipment and made a movie, *The Sands O' Dee.*[6] Other strange events occurred that month. People kept running out of doors to look up at a new sight, young Glenn Martin's "aero-Hydroplane." Martin, who had built his first airplane at Santa Ana two years earlier, flew the pontoon-equipped model to Avalon and back on May 10, 1912. It was the longest over-water flight to

that date, a landmark in the history of aviation.

Martin's experiments over the still waters of Newport Bay were watched with interest throughout the summer. A confident passenger on pioneer flights was his mother, Minta Martin, who clung to the struts as her long skirts flapped in the breeze. Florence Seidel of Santa Ana was one of the first pupils at the Martin Flying School, established in a large tent next door to the East Newport pavilion. Miss Seidel's plane made an unexpected plunge into the bay one day and she spent "five minutes under water" before being rescued by W. S. Collins' son, Lee — and happily revived.

Major Charles McKinstry of the Army Corps of Engineers arrived to supervise the long-awaited survey of the bay, to be done by two men in a rowboat and expected to take about six weeks. Harbor boosters were anxious to give him as good an impression as possible. A dramatic ride in Martin's plane was just the thing! The adventure began with a cruise aboard the Collins launch, *Apolena*. In the middle of the bay McKinstry transferred to the hydroplane for a flight that encircled the bay and landed him at the Balboa pavilion. Shortly afterward James Irvine, who was interested in the survey but unwilling to have harbor lines drawn for the upper bay, arrived in town with General W. H. Bixby, Chief of the Army Corps of Engineers. Irvine and Bixby went for rides over the bay with Martin, viewing the upper bay, "it is thought, with a view of making it a naval base for the government."[7]

On May 10, 1912, aviation pioneer Glenn Martin flew this plane from Newport Bay to Catalina Island, making the longest and fastest over-water flight to that date.

These attempts to impress army engineers with Newport Bay and its potential had been thrilling to watch, but they brought no promises of government improvements or naval installations. Harbor bulkhead and pierhead lines were determined, but confirmation from Washington was delayed several years. Major McKinstry pointed out to local citizens that the government had financed a survey, but that the city must build its own jetties as there was no evidence of commerce that would justify federal expenditure.

W. S. Collins, who had been building boats for several years at his Collins Commercial Company at Balboa, was an increasingly ardent yacht club member. Announcing that he would dredge a motorboat raceway around Balboa Island (the previously-announced automobile raceway never having materialized), he sent to Michigan for a hydroplane boat, the *Balboa Island Flyer II*. The *BIF* deafened residents with its terrible roar as it sped across Newport Bay's few navigable areas, doing a mile in one minute and 32 seconds. In 1913 the Collins Commercial Company built a 51-foot-long motor cruiser to which the Balboa Island developer gave his own initials, calling it the *W.S.* He now owned the largest and fastest boats on the bay. Collins, also a member of the San Joaquin Gun Club, served mallard duck when he honored his employees at an annual banquet in 1913. He assured them that he had "abiding faith" in the future of Newport Bay and had been more successful at "turning sand into money than most people thought possible."[8] *Out West* magazine gave him California-wide fame that year when it published an article on Balboa Island illustrated with a cartoon of Collins inspired by the legend, "Why the Sea is Salt." Collins continued to promise Balboa Island

Inspired by the legend of the magic salt mill "that ground and ground, until the sea was salt," a cartoonist for *Out West* magazine did this sketch of W. S. Collins in 1913. "Mr. Collins," he noted, "has literally made riches from salt water and sand by dredging Newport Bay and making Balboa Island."

needed improvements as well as luxuries that never came. At last he seemed to lose interest in the island of which he had once been so proud. As debts mounted, he began speculating in High Sierra campsites, oil wells on the Newport mesa, and marshlands at Sunset Beach, where he had sent his dredger. Early in 1914, foreclosures on Balboa Island began that were to have repercussions throughout the city.

But the impending economic collapse did not occur until after a gala Fourth of July celebration. Eight banner-decorated automobiles toured the county to distribute 8000 handbills. A band played Sousa marches at the Balboa pavilion for the thousands who came to enjoy the festivities and participate in rowboat and canoe races, three-legged races, sack races, egg races, and dory races through the surf. Forty launches, rowboats, and canoes, all decorated with Japanese lanterns, floated across the bay after dark in a beautiful Illuminated Boat Parade. Highlight of the celebration was the burning of an old hull anchored in the bay: "This will be set on fire and the passengers rescued in the weird light from the burning boat. Two mines will be exploded nearby and a big battle of fireworks from two launches will add excitement to the spectacle." All went off as scheduled; "the boat burned until midnight, when she slipped gently to the bottom."[9]

It was the last big Fourth of July celebration for five years. World War I began a few weeks later. Depression hit all the Newport Bay subdivisions. In 1915 Collins lost the remainder of his Newport Bay holdings, except his castle. George Hart sold 400 acres at Corona del Mar, where only fifteen houses and one small hotel had been built in ten years. East Newport was nearly bankrupt,

West Newport changed hands, Port Orange had collapsed earlier, and the fishermen at the old wharf settlement were poorer than ever. Even gondolier John Scarpa had long since left the scene. When he could not pay for a motorcycle, gun, and "talking machine" bought on the installment plan, his creditors loaded the gondola onto a Pacific Electric car and took it away. Scarpa "beat it back to sunny Italy."[10]

Of all the Newport Bay subdivisions, the one that suffered most in the collapse of 1914-15 was Balboa Island. The seawall of German cement, ranging in height from an inch to over a foot, was crumbling away. Sewer pipes emptying into the bay were exposed at low tide. The beach around the island was tax-delinquent, in danger of being purchased by a private speculator. The island's small park, planted with trees but never dedicated, had been mortgaged and now had a private owner. One day Balboa Island woke up to find itself "awful dry."[11] Collins had collected from residents for water, but failed to pay the city. Forced by circumstances to sell twenty-five Balboa Island lots turned over to him by Collins on an overdue debt, lumber dealer W. W. Crosier accepted $25 apiece.

This drastic decline in real estate values was not the only calamity faced by Newport Beach. Silt and debris began to fill the bay.

Duck Hunting, Yachting, and Aviation

I N EARLY YEARS no dams, levees, and spreading basins controlled the Santa Ana River along its course from the San Bernardino Mountains to the Pacific. In its last few miles before reaching the sea, the river crossed a flood plain between the Newport and Huntington Beach mesas. As it entered the flood plain, the river broke into small channels and disappeared into peat beds covered with willows, tules, water moodies, and vines that made almost impenetrable thickets, known as the "Willows." The Willows served as a sieve, relieving the Santa Ana River waters of silt and sand. Before entering Newport Bay, the water rose again in swamps and Bitter Water Lake, a natural reservoir held in by the sand dunes of the barrier beach. According to Thomas B. Talbert, the river floodwaters "backed and piled up for six hours until the tide went out again. The exit of such a volume of water produced such a tremendous current that it washed out the sedimentary deposits and kept the channels open at Corona del Mar. Otherwise, the whole section of Newport Bay . . . would have remained filled with the debris and silt of the flood waters and would have become another peatland."[1]

Newport Bay, looking west, showing Corona del Mar boat landing at right and Balboa Island at the upper left. About 1913.

Throughout the Mexican and American pioneer periods, firewood had been cut in the Willows. Eventually the area was cleared, drained by ditches, and planted with celery and other crops. But farmers in these peatlands, as well as those in frequently-flooded areas all along the Santa Ana River, objected to the river's ancient habit of overflowing its banks. The "Newbert Protection District" was formed, a channel 300 feet wide made for the river, and levees built. The channel led directly into the west end of Newport Bay.

Engineer D. E. Hughes had remarked in 1909 upon the remarkable stability of Newport Bay, there being virtually no change (except at the entrance) in the 34 years since the first hydrographic survey in 1875. Arthur J. McFadden has stated that according to his father, Robert McFadden, the filtering action of the Willows was so efficient that "the bay was filled up only an inch during the thirty years that he operated it."[2] But by 1912 the newly channeled river had already carried considerable silt into the lower bay. Heavy rains during the first week of March, 1914, choked the channel at the point where it met Newport Bay tidewater with "silt, stumps, and debris of all kinds." Newport Beach realtor C. A. Lancaster said, "Anyone looking over the Bay in its present condition, especially at low tide, can express only a feeling

75

of disgust."[3] Engineer H. Clay Kellogg, director of the flood control work, declared that the river should be diverted from Newport Bay and cut directly into the ocean. Six years were to pass before this was accomplished.

On December 17, 1914, Newport Beach experienced the most destructive storm its earliest residents could remember. Water in the bay rose eight inches above the high tide mark. Ocean swells undermined peninsula houses. Gas and water mains were destroyed, roofs torn off, and boardwalks damaged. Late in April the next year another storm brought floods of water under doors and against store fronts while "rivers of sand ran over the sidewalks and down the streets." It was probably a good time to make the movie, *Sea Spirit of Admiral Jones*. Two Newport Bay launches, five dories, and a number of local fishermen with their nets joined in the "fight at sea," in which "two young men battle in a death struggle, one of them being finally overcome and thrown into the water and left to perish."[4]

The floods brought renewed pressures for harbor improvement. In June, 1915, the California Legislature passed a law enabling city and county to bond themselves for reclamation projects. A few months later the first Orange County Harbor Commission was appointed. Newport Beach banker Lew Wallace, one of its members, led a campaign to win support for a county bond issue. Among those opposed was elderly James McFadden who, in what must have been his last public statement, told a Santa Ana audience that they would be foolish to bond themselves for a project that belonged to the federal government. Local newspapers, however, published a New-

port Harbor prospectus written by Albert Boschke, a civil engineer:

This harbor, having great areas of marsh lands, offers building sites for industrial purposes. By raising this land from six to nine feet above high water with material dredged from channels, industrial property will be created, having its own deep water frontage. This will ultimately result in one of the greatest industrial centers of the Pacific Coast being established at this port, having a frontage of deep water with railroad facilities, fuel oil, and electric power, offering an ideal site that would surely attract great industries. . . .

The great quantity of iron in the neighboring mountains, which is said by men of authority to be of the highest quality, will demand steel plants, rolling mills, and iron works. With such industries will come great shipping yards. Imagine, if you can, a battleship built of iron in a California port. Yet all this is possible and would be very desirable. You have something of importance to offer the government. *Balboa could be made into a naval station, with a dry dock and navy yard.* [italics added.][5]

The industrial possibilities were enough to stagger the imagination. But Newport Beach, a town of about 800 permanent residents beset by economic woes, had one "industry" at the end of 1915. This was the Branagan Glass factory (located between Newport Boulevard and today's Hoag Hospital) which, after several false starts, was making lamp shades and crystal glassware. The concern, hoping to supply a market created when imports from Europe were cut off by World War I, had also made

Ocean front bathhouse damaged by storms, December, 1914.

time. Headlines the next morning in the Santa Ana *Register* proclaimed that the river had entered the ocean at this point, but the means of its doing so was kept a secret for years. A quarter of a mile of tracks, with ties clinging to them, were torn away and swept to sea, followed by "a raging torrent . . . carrying in its swirling flood farm machines, houses, barns, and debris of all descriptions."[6] Not all the flood waters went to sea; much of the deluge entered the bay. The timely sabotage had saved the town, but Newport Bay was badly damaged. Joseph A. Beek wrote:

> The next day the incoming tide could not overcome the flood, with the results that for a time the water flowed neither way, but eddied and swirled about, a southeast wind breaking up the mass of debris and driving it on shore. The water of the bay was the color of chocolate, and the beaches were littered with thousands of oranges and everything else, from decrepit baby buggies to dead calves. A black ooze was deposited wherever the tide reached, piling up in areas of quiet water to a depth of two feet . . . . Many days elapsed before the water clarified. Shellfish, in which the bay then abounded, were smothered by the million, a lot of dredged channels were partially refilled, and the sand bars were converted to mud flats.[7]

enough round globes for new electric street lamps between Newport and Balboa. The globes were shining brightly when, in January 1916, torrential rains damaged the lamp posts and extinguished the lights.

Word came that levees along the Santa Ana River had broken. Flood waters were rising rapidly in the channel that led directly into Newport Bay. This time they would bring tons of debris. Newport Beach appeared doomed. Several local fishermen commandeered an empty Pacific Electric car and ran it down the tracks in the direction of Huntington Beach. They stopped the car near the river channel, took out tools, and began digging a tunnel under the Southern Pacific and Pacific Electric embankments at the edge of the ocean. A trickle of water seeped through the tunnel, and then a little more. The men left just in

OVERLEAF:
Entrance to Newport Bay in 1914, before the jetties were built, showing the east end of the peninsula and a portion of Rocky Point.

Newport Harbor boosters hoped the artificially-created Santa Ana River channel into the ocean would remain open, but county employees closed it to prevent intrusion of salt water into nearby farm lands. A permanent diversion of the river could not be made until county funds were available for repairing the levees, constructing a dam, and building jetties at the new river mouth. While resigned to postponing river diversion, Newport Beach citizens grew increasingly impatient about other aspects of harbor reclamation. Fishermen and yachtsmen alike were weary of the unsafe entrance that prevented their taking boats in and out of the bay. At last the city decided to build one jetty, believing that this demonstration of good faith on its part would surely bring county and federal aid. Even if it did not, they would have one jetty. The cost — $125,000 — would be high for a struggling little town, but on September 25, 1916 they voted the bonds. Lew Wallace made another trip to Washington, Congress finally approved the harbor lines that had been determined four years earlier, and the year ended on a happier note than it had begun.

In mid-December prices at the local theater rose from 15c to 25c for a special showing of *The Lash* and other short movies, a total of nine reels. Filmed at Newport Beach the previous summer, *The Lash* starred several local fisherman. Everyone in town went to watch Henry Starck (who had received $100) pilot a dory through Arch Rock and capsize twice in "angry, foaming waters."On Christmas day the local families, according to custom, "took lunches and all spent the day up at the Palisades (Corona del Mar) gathering abalones, at which they are master hands."[8]

The First Harbor Work /16

ARLY IN 1917 the United States declared war on Germany. While men and boys went off to training camps, Newport Beach began the construction of its first jetty. A temporary railroad was built on a trestle extending 1500 feet out into the ocean from the peninsula point. In September 5000 people celebrated as the first jetty rock was dropped into place. At the end of the year the Orange County Harbor Commission submitted a report recommending the expenditure of $635,-000 for Newport Harbor improvements. At this time German U-boats were preying upon allied shipping in Atlantic waters. Rumor soon spread that the new harbor at Newport would be a submarine base. The Los Angeles *Times* published a large panoramic photograph of the trestle and railroad, announcing that a great harbor would be developed "for government war use and for development of maritime commerce." W. W. Wilson of the financially floundering East Newport Town Company said, "We have the logical base here for submarines and we will give the government all the land it wants and make any improvements suggested to us by government experts."[1] Fortunately for the recreational future of Newport Harbor, World War I ended before Wilson's hopes were realized. When the jetty was completed the city of Newport Beach, impatient at delays in county aid, voted bond issues totalling $115,000 to dredge a "city channel" along the inner shore of the peninsula.

An Orange County bond election was called for June 10, 1919, for $500,000 to divert the Santa Ana River from Newport Bay, lengthen the west jetty built by the city, dredge a "county" channel inside the bay, and build a wharf and railroad spur. Although the work was estimated at $635,000, it was believed that $135,000 worth of dredged materials could be sold to make up the difference. While Lew Wallace and others campaigned to promote a favorable vote, U.S. Navy subchasers *307* and *308* (each 75 feet long and drawing 7½ feet of water) entered the bay to prove that something besides fishing boats could use the newly dredged city channel. On the eve of the election a caravan of automobiles toured northern Orange County towns urging a "yes" vote. The bonds passed, 8622 to 6070. Newport Beach began a gala summer by celebrating. Bands played, three airplanes from March Field looped the loop over the bay, bathing girls paraded in a beauty contest, and free motion pictures were shown at Balboa.

Anchored in Newport Bay in the summer of 1919 was a large barge carrying the superstructure of a "transatlantic liner" that was to be wrecked during the filming of "Wings of the Morning," starring William Farnum

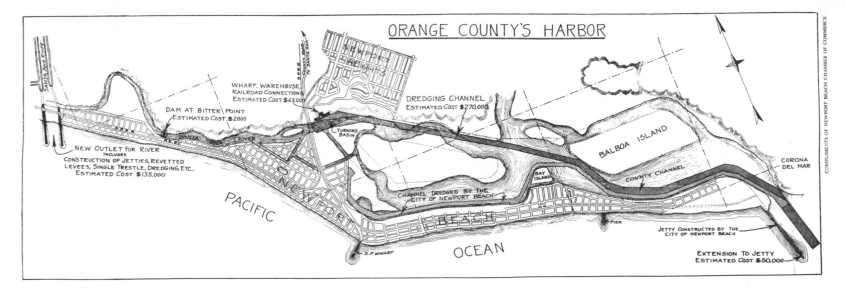

Diagram showing harbor lines as ratified in 1917 and plans for the Orange County harbor work
of 1919-21, including the diversion of the Santa Ana River from the bay.

and Louise Lovely. Nearby a much smaller but more genuine boat, "an oversized rowboat with a kicker," could be seen plying back and forth between Balboa Island and the peninsula. This was Joseph A. Beek's new Balboa Island ferry, the *Ark*. Ferry service to and from the island had been desultory since the collapse of the Collins interests five years ealier, but now a Balboa Island Improvement Association was tackling the many problems facing the potentially beautiful but long neglected island. Beek, who had first seen Balboa Island in 1907 and declared that he would rather live there "in a cottage than exist in a mansion anywhere else," became the island's most enthusiastic lifelong resident.

The *Ark* was soon joined by a second ferry, the *Islander*. Formerly the *Warpy B*, the boat had been wrecked on the bar and abandoned. Beek had towed the craft shore, "on a favorable tide," pumped out the hull, and repainted her. In the meantime, he had revived the annual Illuminated Boat Parade, later renamed by him the Tournament of Lights. By 1920 he was at work on the 20 passenger *Fat Fairy*, 22 feet long and eight feet wide.

In April, 1920, the city of Newport Beach finished its dredging of the city channel (south of Lido Isle). County work began when the first dipper of sand was taken from the county channel (north of Lido). Work was also commenced on twin jetties at the Santa Ana River's proposed new entrance into the ocean beyond West Newport. It was time to engage a harbor master. Joseph A. Beek was the logical choice. Paid $25 a month (for the maintenance of his boat), Beek kept track of vessels entering and leaving the bay, forbade the mooring of boats in the channel, and warned canoes and rowboats to stay out of the way of dredging cables — all the while running the ferry, managing his Balboa Island real estate business, and serving as secretary of the California Senate.

The county dredging of Newport Bay was delayed in the summer of 1920 when a dredger burned. Heavy seas in June, July, and August swept sand from beneath a portion of the city's new west jetty. The rocks began to sink. "A safe entrance is Newport Harbor's most crying need at this time," the Newport *News* said, "and the jetty, flattened by recent storms, should be rebuilt solidly, and at once."[2] Citizens voted $50,000 for repairs. In the meantime the county could not sell much of the dredged material from which it had hoped to realize $135,000. Beek urged Balboa Island residents to accept an offer of dredgings that would have raised the sparsely populated island above its dangerously low level for only $10 or $20 a lot. They declined the offer. Few people had the foresight of James Irvine, the only large buyer of dredged materials at that time. As a result of the deficit in county financing, the commercial wharf and railroad spur were never built. A strip of bayfront land, donated to the city for wharves by James Irvine in 1921, is today the location of the Balboa Bay Club and the Sea Scout Base.

Late in 1920 teams of horses and mules, drawing scrapers, began work on Bitter Point dam, an earth fill 12 feet high, 60 feet wide at the base, and 15 feet wide at the top. At its completion, the Santa Ana River was

The original Newport Beach cannery building, viewed from Thomas Broadway's boatyard in the early 1920s. Built in 1919, the cannery was little used until the mid-1930s when it was bought by Western Canners and remodeled. Today a reproduction of the building houses a restaurant.

Handbill circulated in 1919, at the time of the first Orange County vote on a harbor bond issue. The measure passed, but "commerce" failed to materialize.

at last diverted from Newport Bay. Early the next year the Orange County extension to the west jetty was finished, making the structure 1900 feet long. Since the first dredging at Balboa and East Newport in 1906, $1,505,000 had been spent on Newport Bay by private developers, the city of Newport Beach, and Orange County. It was not enough. The creation of a navigable harbor had only begun. As the need for a second jetty and extensive additional dredging became evident, harbor boosters began to clamor again for federal help. "Who knows a congressman?" asked Lew Wallace. But the answer from Washington had always been the same: *"Where is your commerce?"*

The completion of the first harbor work brought a letdown when commerce did not suddenly and miraculously

develop. As one resident observed, "Many of us, I think, have clung to the belief that ships would literally flock into Newport Harbor as soon as the entrance was made safe and channels dredged. We have hoped for the coming of a Wrigley or someone equally wealthy, who would throw them in and out of port, and all we would be asked to do would be to sit back and raise the price of our real estate."[3] W. A. Irwin, a local realtor, bravely chartered the *Albion*, skippered for the occasion by William Kelley, former pilot at Newport Landing. Newspaper pictures and banner headlines proclaimed that commerce had come to Newport Harbor. "At last," rejoiced the Newport *News*, "a real boat, with real funnels and real smoke pouring out of said funnels."[4] The *Albion* unloaded 100,000 feet of lumber, followed soon afterward by the

Lion with 10,000 feet. This was the last anyone heard of the new commerce, although a Captain Leffingwell brought in a derelict old ship, the *Pokomoke*, with promises to develop trade with San Diego. The *Pokomoke* sank to the bottom of the bay.

Neither Orange County nor the city of Newport Beach provided Harbor Master Beek with markers for the newly dredged city and county channels. Beek found an ingenious substitute. He invented Newport's center channel buoys by inverting two galvanized metal wash tubs, one upon the other, fastening them together through the center, and painting them with black and white vertical stripes. One yachtsman called them "Joe Beek's hat boxes," but the city council, having no higher authority to which to appeal, gave him $300 with which to "clutter

up our channel with these contraptions to his heart's content."[5] Beek, an ardent yachtsman, began to look forward to the regatta of the Southern California Yachting Association, scheduled for Newport Bay late in the summer of 1922.

The regatta of 1922 was not exclusively a yachtsmen's affair. The entire town of Newport Beach prepared to welcome the visitors who soon filled hotels, cottages, rooming houses, and a temporary "tent city." Milk, ice, and bakery wagons made extra deliveries. In a festive atmosphere "men in yachting suits and women in brilliant sport costumes" strolled along the beaches. Duke Kahanamoku, the famous Hawaiian Olympic swimming champion and surfer, arrived and expressed delight at the ideal surfing conditions created by the one jetty, caus-

FAR LEFT:
In July, 1919, Joseph A. Beek began operation of the Balboa Island ferry service with the *Ark*, an "oversized rowboat with a kicker." As years went by, larger passenger and automobile ferries were launched. Once a necessity, the Balboa Island ferry remains today a convenience and source of pleasure to tourists and local residents.

CENTER:
The *Fat Fairy*, built in 1921, was a passenger ferry that pushed an occasional automobile across the bay in this manner.

IMMEDIATE LEFT:
The *Joker*, 1922, was the first self-propelled automobile ferry.

Scene at the Newport Harbor Yacht Club, early 1920s.

ing big breakers to roll in for a long distance. As visiting boats arrived, Harbor Master J. A. Beek, aboard his new sloop *Carrollie,* met them outside the jetty, "putting a pilot aboard each yacht, with instructions where to anchor." The fleet of 200 boats (66 participated in races) was an "impressive sight."[6] Newport Harbor would host many regattas in years to come, but none would ever be remembered as this first one was.

Motion Picture Boats /17

MANY MOTION PICTURES were made on or near Newport Bay in the 1920s. In August, 1922, a visitor noted that "Within a stone's throw of the municipal pier . . . a perfectly good missionary has been burned at the stake — at least very badly treated, huts have been burned to the ground; scores of hard-boiled seamen have tried to scuttle a freighter and have made their getaways in long, low, rakish-looking craft." Newport Bay had many attractions for Hollywood producers — the still waters of the bay, ocean surf, the rocky cliffs and caves of Corona del Mar, long empty beaches, sand dunes, and unpopulated countryside. The trip from Los Angeles took only an hour by Pacific Electric; equipment could be sent by flat car. Newport and Balboa boat builders were always ready to construct new boats or remodel old ones. Although movie making began at Newport as early as 1912, and possibly sooner, the first important production was the 1917 version of *Cleopatra*.

Early in the summer of that year eighty men began to construct a fleet of twenty-nine ships on the peninsula near Balboa. Crowds of fascinated visitors watched the building of the *triremes*, galleys of ancient design, for the filming of *Cleopatra* with silent screen vampire Theda Bara in the lead. Bystanders could not believe their ears when told that all the strange and beautiful vessels were to be burned in the upper bay, except Cleopatra's ship which was to be dashed to pieces at Rocky Point. What lavish and wasteful expenditure! When the ships were ready Cleopatra, Antony, and their company arrived by Pacific Electric and pitched tents on the sand.

When the day came for filming the historic battle of Actium (waged in the Adriatic, off the coast of Greece), hundreds of people lined the low road around the east side of the upper bay. Cameramen stood on the cliffs or waited in small boats on the water. At the sound of a trumpet the triremes of Cleopatra and Antony swept into the upper bay, each propelled by a row of sixty brawny oarsmen at the front and a carefully concealed Newport Bay launch at the rear. Among those on board were a number of Newport Beach fishermen suitably costumed with shields, helmets, swords, tunics, and sandals. As few actors could swim, the fishermen were to enact the dangerous roles requiring falling or being thrown into the bay.

The opposing Roman forces, seven hundred strong, straggled down the west banks of the upper bay. Unlike Cleopatra's and Mark Antony's men they had not come on the Red Cars, but by Southern Pacific, disembarking at the nearby Paularino siding. One reporter thought they looked like rejects from Uncle Sam's army. "Some were

short and some were tall, some knock-kneed and some bow-legged. Others were pigeon-toed, and some were suffering from flatfoot. Several of them looked so hard and tough that their faces must have ached. One old fellow tottered up the hill, and it seemed that the gentle breeze which was blowing would topple him over into the bay. Another Roman gladiator, with lead-pencil legs, looked like he might have been borrowed from a museum . . . . These were the men who defeated Antony and Cleopatra in that memorable battle.''

When the fight at sea was over, and the Newport fishermen had swum ashore, the victorious Romans prepared for the next scene. They drenched all the ancient ships except Cleopatra's with 5000 gallons of crude oil, tossing on hay and other flammable material. All this, when ablaze, produced ''one of the most magnificent and spectacular scenes ever taken on the water.'' Cleopatra's galley, as it lay on the shore of the upper bay that night, was robbed of its sails and ''jewels and costumes worth $1000.''[1]

Two years later, in August, 1919, the barkentine *Fremont* approached Newport Bay under full sail. This old ship, built in Philadelphia in 1852, had been declared unseaworthy after long years of service on the high seas and assigned to the less glorious task of being a movie boat. According to the Newport *News*, she had been remodeled by the Goldwyn Movie Corporation to represent the *Hispaniola* in the first filming of *Treasure Island*. Now she was being given a new superstructure by the

In 1919 the old barkentine *Fremont*, used in motion picture work went, on the sandbar in the entrance to Newport Bay and was later dynamited.

Wilson Brothers of Balboa for a Capital Company motion picture. Although "200 feet long and drawing ten feet of water," the *Fremont* entered the bay without difficulty. "Plenty of water was found at all points along the entire length of the channel," the local newspaper stated, "and the old vessel, scarred by many a stormy sea, weather-beaten, and baked by the sun of various climes, rides peacefully at anchor."[2]

On October 14 the *Fremont*, with 45 persons aboard, went to sea for a day of filming. At the time of her return "a swift current was running out to sea." The Wilson Brothers did not wish to tow her back through the entrance with the boats available. But the ship sprang a leak. Most of the actors aboard could not swim. The vessel carried only one small dory. At the insistence of the movie makers, the *Fremont* was towed in by four boats, manned by fisherman Al Dixon and three other men. Although "the boys hung on to the big boat with grim determination, the odds against them were too heavy, and when a large swell hit the helpless tub she all but wrecked those who would save her."[3] The old three-master went on the bar. The frightened actors, with but one dim lantern, spent a harrowing night on board. They were rescued the following morning, one at a time, on lines stretched from the rocks at Corona del Mar. Each succeeding tide drove the *Fremont* higher on the bar. Several days later she was dynamited. Shots of the explosion were used in motion pictures for several years afterwards.

Newport Bay swarmed with pirates early in 1924, for the filming of *Captain Blood*, starring J. Warren Kerrigan. Two old sailing ships, the *Prosper* and the *Taurus*, were remodeled near the Balboa pavilion. The *Taurus*, said

The 50-passenger *Limit*, launched in 1916 by the East Newport Town Company, frequently served as camera boat for early movies.

Prosper and *Taurus*, 1924, being remodeled at the pavilion for use in the motion picture *Captain Blood*.

Closeup of *Prosper* and *Taurus*, showing details of remodeling.

to have been "hogged by overloading," was towed down the coast from San Francisco. But the *Prosper*, a veteran of twenty years in the Alaska trade, sailed into the bay under her own canvas. Her Danish skipper, Captain Sorensen, 67, remained in command of the reconditioned vessel throughout the filming of the movie. It was understood that the *Taurus* would be burned when the picture was completed. Sorensen hoped the seaworthy *Prosper* would be re-rigged and put back into use. "There are a good many more years of good service in that ship,"[4]

he said. But both vessels were sent to the bottom of the sea off the Catalina isthmus.

Although countless motion pictures have been made in the Newport Harbor area through the years, the unpopulated beaches and sand dunes that attracted the first film makers did not last long. As early as 1931 H. L. Sherman wrote that "present developments have raised too many houses, electric light poles, and wharves to permit 'shooting' of scenes which call for primitive conditions."[5]

Cleopatra's galley, motion picture boat built at East Newport in 1917 for the first movie version of *Cleopatra*. House in background stood on Corona del Mar bluff.

After the filming of *Cleopatra*, this picturesque but fragile craft went aground on the bar in the entrance to Newport Bay and was soon battered to pieces. View from peninsula point looking across toward Corona del Mar bluffs.

Crossing the Newport Bar in the 1920's /18

THE OVERALL harbor picture was discouraging at the beginning of 1923. The one jetty was neither high enough nor long enough. The sandbar in the entrance was growing larger. Channels dredged inside the bay had become shallow. Harbor boosters urged the employment of one capable individual to work full-time to obtain federal and county help for the needed improvements. The task was given to British-born Harry Welch, who became secretary of a newly organized Orange County Chamber of Commerce in the spring of 1923. Late in that year he went to Washington D.C. with a group of Orange County civic leaders, to try to obtain federal help. Results were encouraging. At a hearing in Los Angeles in 1924, army engineers recommended a federal appropriation of $630,000 for Newport Harbor improvements. But nothing ever came of it. As H. L. Sherman wrote, "The U.S. Government will further improve a port already possessed of commerce, but it will not do the initial work to bring commerce to a harbor which has not previously enjoyed it."[1] Harry Welch faced a gigantic task, one that would take thirteen years to

complete. His devotion to the cause and his accomplishments are remembered today by the Harry Welch Park at Newport Dunes, named in his honor.

Lew Wallace and George T. Peabody, harbor boosters, had long looked forward to the reclamation of Pacific Electric Island (later Lido). Together they persuaded oil man W. K. Parkinson to buy the island for $45,000 and finance its dredging and filling at a cost of $261,000. Parkinson supplied the funds but the man who directed this early Lido Isle work was George T. Peabody, son of a pioneer Newport Beach family. His father, Henry A. Peabody, editor of the Santa Ana *Blade* and postmaster at Santa Ana, had opened a store on the Newport ocean front in the 1890s. Young George, who grew up to be "one of the most picturesque individuals in the great Southwest,"[2] worked in the store and delivered ice to customers. As a young man in his twenties, he was instrumental in the incorporation of Newport Beach and became one of the most knowledgeable harbor boosters. Studying harbors in other parts of the country, he recognized the potential of the future Lido Isle as the nucleus of a great commercial harbor. Plans for the island's shape had been made in 1912 when harbor lines were determined. Under the direction of Peabody it was filled in 1923-24 to eleven feet above the high tide line.

Star boats at 1926 regatta of the Southern California Yachting Association.

The narrow, dangerous entrance to Newport Bay photographed on May 27, 1923, showing the first west jetty and a large sandbar.

boat operators who went in and out of it regularly. The jetty continued to sink. Navigational lights were needed.

It was not until the fall of 1923 that a bell buoy was anchored seaward of the jetty. In December of that year the Lighthouse Service furnished jetty lights and helped Beek install them. He recalled that it was a dangerous task, necessitating the pouring of concrete platforms on which to mount the lights. The ferry *Islander* pushed a barge loaded with sand, gravel, and cement, out to the end of the jetty where a white acetylene light was installed. Another light was placed at the shore end of the jetty, and a red one on the Corona del Mar bluffs. Placed in charge of these lights and the terrible pathway they marked was Antar Deraga, Russian-born meteorologist who had come to Newport Beach in 1919 while the first harbor work was under way. Deraga and his wife, Martha, deeply tanned people fond of the out of doors, lived in a small house on the Corona del Mar cliffs. Deraga used colored lights at night and flag signals in the daytime to inform mariners of storm warnings telephoned from Los Angeles. H. L. Sherman wrote that "in addition to the storm warning devices, which were intelligible to all seafaring men, a set of local signals was devised to give notice of unsafe conditions at the harbor entrance."

Deraga owned a fine collection of meteorological instruments, making the Corona del Mar station one of the best equipped in California. He made observations and recordings for the Scripps Institute of Oceanography at La Jolla, results of which he mailed to the institute each month. Fascinated by the new science of aeronautics, he was the first to encourage the establishment of an Orange County airport. Eventually he left Newport Beach and became a professor of meteorology at California

But dreams of wharves and railroad terminals on Lido Isle were far from realization in 1923. Harry Welch had gone to work, but his long crusade on behalf of Newport Harbor was only beginning. In the meantime, the dangerous condition of the entrance was a matter of constant concern to Harbor Master Beek and to the fishermen and

Institute of Technology. But in 1923 he had self-appointed tasks at Corona del Mar. On New Year's Day three persons drowned when their boat capsized in the bay entrance. Deraga, the only man in Newport Beach familiar with resuscitation methods, worked over the victims for several hours, but without avail. A Life Saving Corps was formed, with Deraga as captain. He was provided with a surf dory. Additional life saving equipment, representing a total investment of $329.74, included lines and small buoys to be used in rescue work. These few items proved hopelessly inadequate.

On June 8, 1924, thirteen persons were washed off the fishing launch *Adieu* when it capsized. Skipper Guy Perkins had approached the entrance "during one of the deceptive lulls that are characteristic of ground swell behavior."[3] He said he felt the boat "go up and up, and that it seemed as if it would never come down. Feeling how helpless he was, he jumped into the ocean. The vessel turned upside down and was crushed."[4] Perkins swam safely ashore. Deraga and the Life Saving Corps worked for three hours to save the other twelve victims. They resuscitated four. Eight were drowned. Yachtsman H. B. Webster said a few days later of the bay entrance, "We are inclined too much to play down its dangers . . . there is not a mother's son of us who has not repeatedly confessed a wholesome dread of the bar and admitted that it might at some time get him."[5]

Jetty repairs were badly needed, but there seemed no way to finance them. Army engineers examined the deteriorating structure and found a "grave menace . . . the breakwater slowly pounding to pieces and in dire need of repairing . . . The jetty rocks have either sunk or been washed aside . . . Waves pound through the breakwater and deposit sand in the channel. This has resulted in gradually filling in the entrance, thereby proving a serious menace to craft coming in and out. Erosion has been going on many months. There are now several huge gaps. The bar is getting larger. All kinds of boats are having difficulty."[6]

Disappointed in their attempts to obtain federal aid, Harry Welch and the second Orange County Harbor Commission, appointed in 1924, engaged General Lansing Beach, retired chief of the Army Corps of Engineers, to prepare a complete survey of reclamation work needed

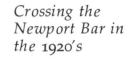

Crossing the Newport Bar in the 1920's

The entrance was dangerous, but the bay was serene. Looking northwest with Balboa Island at right and the upper bay in the distance.

The first 1900-foot west jetty, built jointly by Newport Beach and Orange County, looked like this by July 15, 1925. Army engineers had found it "a grave menace . . . the breakwater slowly pounding to pieces and in dire need of repairing."

at Newport Harbor and an estimate of costs. Beach's report recommended an expenditure of $1,200,000 for extending and enlarging the west jetty, building an east jetty from the rocky point at Corona del Mar, a complete dredging of the lower bay, and raising land wherever possible. The upper bay, he said, might "be developed into an industrial harbor, its logical use." As to the recreational possibilities of the area, he said, "Provide some accommodation for yachts. Men who own yachts are usually keen businessmen with eyes open for opportunity."[7] Welch and the Harbor Commission began the long

months of groundwork necessary to bring the matter before Orange County voters. While they pursued this task, a new obstruction appeared in the bay entrance.

Newport Beach fisherman Rube Shafer bought the *Muriel*, a large movie ship, and converted her into a mackerel barge to be anchored out in the ocean. In May, 1925, while being towed out of the bay, the *Muriel* stuck fast in the entrance. While she would shift about from time to time, never in the next five years did anyone succeed in removing this new hazard to navigation.

Duke Kahanamoku, one of the members of Antar Deraga's Life Saving Corps, organized a surfing club with headquarters at a bath house on the beach at Corona del Mar. Here members kept their long, heavy mahogany surfboards. On June 14, 1925, when entrance conditions were similar to those met by the *Adieu* a year earlier, Deraga saw the launch *Thelma* approaching. From the bluffs he waved to its occupants to turn back, but they did not. Kahanamoku, having awakened in his tent on the beach, was about to take a morning dip when he saw the boat capsize. Seventeen men were thrown into the churning waters. The Hawaiian surfing champion dashed into the mountainous swells with his board, and in three trips saved seven victims. Deraga and Charley Plummer, following Kahanamoku's example, took boards on which they rescued five more, but five men drowned. The heroic work by the three rescuers was the first convincing demonstration anywhere of the usefulness of the surfboard or paddleboard in life saving. For a number of years afterward boards were standard life saving equipment.

High surf pounded the jetty throughout the day of the *Thelma* disaster. By afternoon the government's

The *Muriel,* a motion picture ship converted for use as a mackerel fishing barge, broke her tow lines and went on the sandbar in the bay entrance. Shown here on August 1, 1925, she remained a hazard to navigation for the next five years.

Entrance conditions had little effect upon yachting inside the bay, where increasing numbers of summer residents owned every kind of boat that could navigate its shallow waters. In addition to the Newport Harbor Yacht Club, there were now two new clubs, the Southland Sailing Club (later the Balboa Yacht Club), and the Balboa Island Yacht Club. Headquarters for the Balboa Island Yacht Club, for young sailors aged four to sixteen, was the beach in front of the South Bay Front home of its founders, Mr. and Mrs. Joseph A. Beek. Aware of the need of waterfront education for children, the Beeks sponsored a program which, continued today, includes swimming, diving, paddleboard paddling, rowing, sailing, and picnics. Many of Newport Harbor's most experienced yachtsmen had their first sailing experiences as members of this club.

By 1926 the rapidly growing local sailing fleet included three Stars, twelve Marions, five Sea Mews, seven Flappers, and sixteen Snowbirds. Among the Newport boat builders were Thomas Broadway, G. V. and Mark Johnson, Ben Cope, and Donald Douglas. A building boom was under way on Balboa Island and all along the peninsula, touched off by the completion earlier that year of the long-awaited coast highway from Long Beach to Newport Beach. The road was to be extended to Laguna Beach and a bridge built across the upper bay, ending the long isolation of Corona del Mar. But the two most important events of the year 1926 were a bond election and a regatta.

Orange County citizens were to vote on June 10 in an election of the utmost importance to the future of Newport Harbor. The proposed bond issue of $1,200,000 for harbor improvements, culmination of almost three

expensive light on the inner end of the jetty was loose, swaying back and forth. Crowds watched as Plummer climbed a line to take down the light and hand it to Deraga, who lowered it to the rocks. Later that year a heavy storm wrecked the Life Saving Corps' only boat, the dory used by Deraga for rescue work of all kinds. Help came, however, as a result of General Lansing Beach's pleas to the Lighthouse Service following his survey of Newport Bay earlier that year. "At considerable expense," the Service "installed new lights, ranges, and buoys throughout the entire navigable portion of lower Newport Bay, these installations to be in charge of Antar Deraga."[8]

years' work by Harry Welch and others, was hotly contested. Proponents argued that a great commercial harbor would bring added prosperity to Orange County's agricultural economy. Ranchers responded that they had voted for a commercial harbor in 1919 and seen no tangible results. A recreational harbor, they feared, would mainly benefit vacationers from outside of Orange County. While Newport businessmen still hoped for a commercial harbor, yachtsmen and summer home owners would have preferred a recreational one but were willing to vote on any measure that would make the entrance safe and deepen the channels. The election was close, but the bonds were defeated. "Farmers Kill Harbor," announced headlines in the Newport *News*. It was a crushing blow to the harbor boosters.

During the week before the election, eight persons had been rescued from drowning in the entrance, Antar Deraga stated that since the beginning of the year he had continually turned back boats seeking to leave the bay. He said, "The defective entrance is a source of constant worry to mariners . . . Every sea-going man gives the place a black eye."[9] A month after the failure of the county bond issue James and George Jr., teen-aged sons of Mr. and Mrs. George A. Rogers of Los Angeles, took three young friends for a ride one day in their Dodge motor boat. As the boys approached the harbor entrance, Deraga called and waved at them to turn back. The boys disregarded his warnings. Their boat went through the entrance, around the bell buoy, and capsized as it started back in. Four youths were rescued, but George Rogers Jr., 16, a polio victim who wore heavy leg braces, sank from sight and drowned.

The defeat of the harbor bonds, followed by this tragedy, put Harbor Master Beek in a cautious mood as the 1926 regatta approached. He now owned a new harbor patrol and pilot boat, the 30-foot *Vamos*, built a year earlier. Already her bronze towing bitt had "pulled many a boat off the sand bar and out of the breakers." Beek (also Newport Harbor Yacht Club Commodore at this time), wrote later:

> This regatta occurred at a time when the harbor entrance was in its worst condition. The west jetty had failed, the east jetty was only a project, and the inlet channel was almost completely blocked by sand bars. The situation was met by the anchoring of a large barge in the ocean near the bell buoy on which was erected an enormous sign saying "Take a Pilot." This sign was illuminated by ten 500-candle-power Coleman lanterns so that it could be seen for miles in the darkest night. Pilot boats, tow boats, shore boats, and Reception Committee boats were in evidence at all times of the day and night. The Commodore anchored his cruiser *Vamos* in the ocean not far from the pilot barge and slept there each night during the regatta, getting up whenever a bomb on the pilot barge announced the arrival of a visitor. A pilot was put aboard each visiting yacht and a pilot boat preceded the visitor into the bay.[10]

The regatta was an outstanding event, with 631 yachts participating and no casualties. Orange County citizens returned to the polls in December, 1926, to vote on a smaller Newport Harbor bond proposal than the one defeated the previous June. Orange County voters also turned down the second issue, which would have financed an east jetty and entrance dredging. As in 1917, the city of Newport Beach decided to undertake harbor work on its own. In February, 1927, voters endorsed a bond issue of $500,000 for an east jetty and an extension to the original west one. It was understood that the work would be done under the direction of army engineers, and that the new jetty would be built of rock according to plans drawn by General Lansing Beach.

When work began, citizens were surprised to learn that the project was not being done by army engineers, but by the Newport Beach city engineer. Working on a commission basis, he designed and constructed an east jetty of reinforced concrete instead of rock. The extension to the west jetty was of rock, as specified by General Beach, but it curved in such a way as to cause erosion along the peninsula beach, undermining ocean-front houses. Santa Ana newspapers published numerous attacks against the city of Newport Beach, while the entrance between the old jetty and the new one refused to "scour." The sandbar grew larger than ever. All the $500,000 had been spent. No money remained for dredging. Clearly the engineering had been faulty. Hundreds flocked to the scene to watch breakers wash away the Balboa beach. H. L. Sherman wrote, "The impression was being broadcast that the city of Newport Beach was in a hopeless dilemma with respect to the improvement and maintenance of its harbor entrance."[11]

The defective work was embarrassing as well as disheartening to a resort city that had expected the summer of 1928 to be the greatest in its history. Newport Harbor had at last achieved recognition in national yachting circles. The Transpacific race to Honolulu was scheduled to leave from the harbor entrance at the end of May.

The International Star races were scheduled for August, the first time they had ever been held on the west coast. Thousands of cars would be coming to Newport Beach on the coast highway. The new Rendezvous Ballroom was open. Harbor Island, developed by Joseph A. Beek and Louis Briggs, was on the market with the strictest building restrictions of any Newport Bay beachfront

Crossing the Newport Bar in the 1920's

Rebuilding the west jetty, June, 1927.

property to that date. Houses were to cost at least $5000. Significant plans for Lido Isle were also announced. It was to be a residential island, in spite of the original developer's hope of a base for commercial harbor installations.

How could Newport Harbor host the beginning of the Transpacific race and the International Star regatta when the depth of the water over the sandbar in the entrance was four feet at low tide? To meet the emergency, Joseph A. Beek relinquished his post as Harbor Master, turning it over to his assistant, Thomas Jay, in order to serve full time as chairman of a newly organized Citizens' Harbor Committee. With money raised from private donations, including pennies from school children, the committee engaged the small dredger *Little Aggie* for ten thousand dollars' worth of dredging. Beek's patrol boat *Vamos* worked along with the *Little Aggie,* taking soundings and towing her back into the bay on one occasion when she broke her moorings and began to drift to sea.

Work was completed in time for the Memorial Day beginning of the Transpacific race, in which six yachts left for Hawaii. Newport Beach, with a permanent population of about 2000, prepared to welcome Star boat owners from the east coast. Few of them knew what to expect in the wild west, "an almost virgin territory from a yachting angle." Visitors were pleased with the eleven-mile offshore course and the Pacific's dependable westerly breezes. In addition to the yachting races of 1928, another event of that summer was long remembered. Duke Kahanamoku's Surfing Club at Corona del Mar, twelve wooden boards strong, hosted the "Surfboard Championship of the World."

Crossing the Newport Bar in the 1920's

This photograph of the rebuilt west jetty and the new short east jetty, taken April 12, 1928, shows the entrance full of sand and rock dumped along the peninsula ocean front to prevent further erosion.

The Depression Brings a Surprise /19

AFTER THE emergency harbor entrance dredging in 1928, Newport Beach employed a new city engineer, Richard L. Patterson, who had participated earlier in the first Orange County harbor work done in 1920-21 by Leeds and Barnard of Los Angeles. Confident of Patterson's ability, citizens endorsed a bond issue of $200,000 for corrective work at the harbor entrance, including the blasting away of the *Muriel* and the construction of rock groins to prevent further beach erosion. When the work was completed the entrance was safer, but careful pilots stayed close to the west jetty where the channel was deeper. Newport Bay had not yet become Newport Harbor. Longer jetties, a deeper entrance, and complete dredging of the lower bay were needed. The hope of federal help for these improvements seemed farther away than ever, for it was clear

by now that Newport's future was as a yachting and recreational harbor. The U.S. government did not finance pleasure ports.

For years Newport Beach had over-taxed citizens for harbor projects. Now other matters needed the attention of the city engineer. There were sewer systems to install, streets and sidewalks to pave, and bridges to build. The largest municipal project, undertaken in 1930, was the paving and installation of then-unique underground utilities for Lido Isle. Following the dredging and filling of the island in 1923-24, it had lain undeveloped for several years. The defeat of Orange County harbor bonds in 1926 ended owner W. K. Parkinson's dream of the island as a base for the wharves and industrial installations of a commercial harbor. After Parkinson's death in 1927, his widow sold an interest in the island to William Clarke Crittenden who employed John P. Elsbach of Los Angeles to subdivide it and sell lots. As architectural planner Elsbach engaged Swiss architect Franz Herding, a man familiar with the French and Italian Rivieras. Herding had also visited new waterfront developments in Florida. He designed an elliptical drive around the island and a number of short, parallel inside streets. These *vias* were given French, Italian, and Spanish place names. Houses were to be of Mediterranean architecture, tile-roofed,

Newport Harbor entrance, following federal reclamation projects of 1934-36. Work (begun in January, 1935) included the removal of approximately 8,500,000 tons of sand and 50,000 tons of rock. The 750-acre water area of the lower bay was dredged to a depth of 10 feet, anchorage area to 15 feet, main channel to 20 feet, and entrance channel to 25 feet. Approximately 210,000 tons of rock were used to extend the west jetty to 2830 feet and the east jetty to 1673 feet. Newport Harbor was dedicated on May 23, 1936.

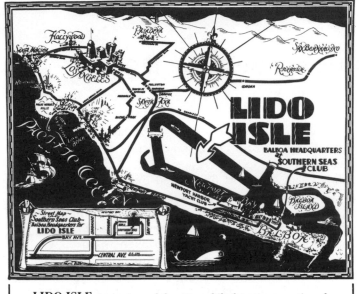

LIDO ISLE is easy to reach by automobile from every section of Southern California. The shortest route from Los Angeles is via Ninth Street and Telegraph Road through Santa Fe Springs, Norwalk, Buena Park, and Huntington Beach. Study the map for other routes.

Page from Lido Isle promotional pamphlet, 1928.

with walled patio gardens. A high tower on the new clubhouse looked out over a bare sand island — destined, according to the promotional brochure, to be "modeled after the *Lido*, the exquisite Italian resort on the Adriatic at Venice." Here, it was said, "the elite and fashionable of continental Europe foregather to introduce the newest styles and fashion in beach sport costumes."[1]

No bridge led to Lido Isle in the summer of 1928 when prospective lot purchasers enjoyed free lunches and *Chris-Craft* rides across the bay. Crittenden and his representatives installed temporary utilities and began to build half a dozen model houses. But no one wanted bayfront lots at $6200 and up in 1928. At the end of the year Crittenden pleaded with the city of Newport Beach to install streets and utilities under the 1911 Improvement Act, making the cost a lien against each lot. The mayor accused him of trying to stampede the city council. "Can the city make Lido bloom overnight and bring prosperity to Newport?"[2] he asked. In spite of the mayor's reservations and the stock market crash of October, 1929, the city awarded a contract for the $1,222,861 Lido Isle improvement project to the Griffith Company early in 1930. Included were underground utilities, light posts, streets, curbs, and broad walkways. The completion of this contract, largest of its kind ever let in California to that time, did nothing to spur sales of Lido Isle lots. At the end of 1930 Crittenden relinquished his interest in the island. Ownership of the 105-acre tract, encumbered by improvement bonds and delinquent taxes, reverted to the Title Insurance and Trust Company of Los Angeles.

Lido Isle developers, from the beginning, had tried to avoid all the mistakes made by W. S. Collins in the creation of Balboa Island. But they had not anticipated a financial depression. The Title Insurance and Trust Company formed an Assets Liquidation Corporation, opened headquarters in a tent on the sand, and prepared to "liquidate" Lido Isle. Prices were slashed to about a fifth of what they had been previously. By July 23, 1931, it was announced that the half million dollar mark had been reached in the giant liquidation sale, but most of the island remained unsold. There were, however, brighter aspects to the Lido Isle picture in 1931. Bicyclists enjoyed the wide paved streets with a sweeping view of the bay. On the evening of the Tournament of Lights thousands parked cars on Lido Isle streets and watched the illuminated boat parade from its shores.

Depression did not dampen enthusiasm for the annual Tournament of Lights. Everyone looked forward to the tournament, but the children who participated enjoyed it most. With one or two exceptions the Tournament of Lights was directed by Joseph A. Beek from 1919 through 1949. (The event was not held during World War II). Writing his *Balboa Island Yarns* in 1950, Beek recalled:

> There is no music so lovely as the voices of happy children, and there is something very appealing about these same voices when floating across the water come such plaintive messages as, "My tow line broke. Will you take me up to my tow boat?" or, "Some of my candles have gone out. Please help me light them."
>
> . . . As one tournament followed another, schemes of decoration were as varied as the imagination of youth. No matter what the plan or how unsuccessfully it was carried out, the result was always pleas-

The narrow peninsula ocean beach, shown here, was considerably widened during the federal harbor work of 1934-36.

ing. Boats are beautiful, so are lights reflected by the water, so are children. Float these lovely things on the placid surface of our tranquil bay, with a moon overhead, or fire works flashing in the sky. Add to this romantic music and the cadence of youthful voices and you have something so lovely that it is no wonder the world came by the thousands and finally by the hundreds of thousands to see it.[3]

Through the years there were floats depicting nursery rhymes, songs, fairy tales, Bible stories, sea caverns, ancient ships, animal life, and even a church with lighted windows and a boat bell in its steeple. Ed Ainsworth has described the beginning of a Tournament of Lights, led according to tradition by the *Vamos:* "A star shell broke forth in a glistening burst in the sky, sending the leaders of the fleet into action. As the boats started forth music began to skim across the water from guitars and mandolins in Spanish orchestras. Giant searchlights swept the heavens. Lights began to be seen everywhere, each one boasting its scintillating twin in the calm waters, and then the Tournament of Lights parade — ethereal, brilliant, and gliding — came wafting down the bay."[4]

Eventually the Tournament of Lights drew such crowds of people to Newport Beach that it had to be discontinued. No longer were there places to park or waterfront vacant lots from which to watch the parade. But in 1931 there had been plenty of room. By 1932 there were 38 houses on Lido Isle and 800 boats in the bay, many of them for sale. The economic picture was gloomy at the beginning of 1933. "Most of us are at the bottom of our resources and many are there who have gone beyond that," wrote Sam Meyer of the Newport *News* as the year opened.[5]

Fishing boats lay idle. Many Newport families' cooking and heating gas had been shut off because of unpaid bills. The city council slashed payrolls asking, "How are we going to keep our schools open?"[6] Wages were 25c an hour for those lucky enough to find jobs. The Roosevelt administration began in March. Banks closed. On March 10, 1933, the Long Beach earthquake damaged Newport's only grade school, toppled chimneys, and cracked streets and curbs. It was the lowest ebb in the city's history.

Harbor improvement, long a dead issue, had never been forgotten by Los Angeles resident George A. Rogers, whose polio-crippled son had drowned in the bay entrance in the summer of 1926. Rogers, a wealthy retired rock contractor and highway builder, had many friends in government circles. As soon as he read the provisions of the Roosevelt administration's National Recovery Act that were intended to create employment, he grasped the possibilities of obtaining funds to develop a recreational harbor. Another who had not forgotten the harbor issue was city engineer Richard L. Patterson. When Rogers and Patterson asked the city council to send them to Washington, the council was skeptical and the mayor voted "no." Newport Beach was so poor that tickets to Washington for what seemed a wild goose chase were an unnecessary extravagance. Harbor boosters had gone to Washington before, without success. But at last the city bought Patterson a ticket. Rogers paid his own way.

City engineer Patterson estimated that the extension and rebuilding of the jetties, plus a last big dredging, would cost $1,830,000. He and Rogers first won the endorsement of the Army Corps of Engineers, who recommended that the federal government finance half the cost, or $915,000. The next step, approval by the Public Works Administration, was gained with the help of Senators William G. McAdoo and Hiram Johnson who persuaded Harold L. Ickes, Secretary of the Interior, to allocate an additional $230,000 in federal funds, leaving a balance of $640,000 to be raised by an Orange County bond election. When Rogers and Patterson arrived home, along with harbor booster A. B. Rousselle who had joined them in Washington, the news of the federal grant was received with wild rejoicing. It was incredible that federal help for Newport Harbor should arrive in the middle of a depression! Patterson, Rogers, Rousselle, Harry Welch, and others worked long hours to promote the bond election. In 1933 Orange County citizens, including the farmers, voted "yes." The harbor project would bring employment. The bond issue passed.

Delays followed. In the Washington confusion of many applications for PWA and WPA funds, a portion of the Newport Harbor grant was transferred elsewhere. It looked as if Orange County voters had been tricked into voting $640,000, believing the federal government would furnish the other $1,190,000. George Rogers boarded the train again. Harry Welch later wrote: "George Rogers, well along in years, worn from the stress and difficulties of the bond campaign, was now a sick man. But with that determination that had built his fortune, he turned down all appeals, and headed back into the chill February of Washington. Despite the doctor's orders to return to sunny California, Rogers made the weary rounds of political officials; days extended into weary weeks, weeks into grim months." When at last he succeeded in having the funds restored, Rogers returned home to a tumultuous welcome. He was the hero of the hour. After forty-six years of fruitless attempts, Newport Harbor had at last won a federal appropriation.

Directed by army engineers, the last dredging began early in 1935. Ed Ainsworth, writing a generation before the ecological concerns of the 1960s, whimsically suggested that thousands of birds gathered near the bay entrance might object:

> Just think of it . . . these new fangled people are going to send dredgers in here and just raise cain with our roosts. There won't be a mudflat left in Newport Bay. It's a crime. This new pleasure harbor, the first pleasure harbor on the Pacific Coast, is going to be fine for everyone except the birds. The whole bay is going to be at least ten feet deep.
>
> The dredgers are almost unbelievably powerful. They have rotators at the end. They plunge down into the muck and ooze at the bottom and agitate it powerfully. As the mud boils up it is caught by powerful pumps and sucked into pipes. This is the ingenious part. The pipes lead where it has been decided to dump the silt. Some of it will be carried a mile or so over to the mainland. It will be dumped along the shore. There will be so much of it that it will build up the marshlands into habitable lots . . . Even the fishing boat section of the harbor will be changed. The unsightly little craft will move farther up the bay, away from the snooty yachts . . . From here you can tell what a thrill yachtsmen will get entering the beautiful harbor. But it certainly is hard on the birds. I hope they can find some nice mudflats somewhere else.[7]

The dredger *John McMullen* in the entrance channel below
the Corona del Mar bluffs, 1935.

It was while the harbor dredging was going on that
long-neglected West Newport began to show new signs
of life. Ralph Maskey was the leader in this development,
urging the city to dredge the old canals that had been
filled with silt and sand in the floods of 1914-16. Newport
Island was built up to eleven feet above high tide.
Unsightly oil derricks were removed. In 1935 Paul A.
Palmer arrived to take on an assignment at which others
had failed — the sale of Lido Isle lots. In 1933 the Griffith
Company had bought 750 Lido lots, leaving the Title
Insurance and Trust Company with a few more than one
hundred to dispose of. Palmer estimated that he could
sell the lots belonging to the two companies in five years.
It was to take him nearly twenty.

As dredging and jetty construction continued, many
new boats entered the bay, among them George Rogers'
large motor yacht *Norconian* which he renamed the
Memory in honor of his son.

At Easter, local controversies arose over "Bal Week,"
the annual influx of young people who found plenty of
cottages for rent and usually had a rousing good time
but sometimes committed acts of vandalism. Mackerel
fishing began to flourish as Western Canners moved into
Newport's old cannery building that had stood on the
"Rhine" since the 1920s. Newport Harbor began a new
tradition in 1935 with the Flight of the Snowbirds, an
annual young people's sailing event that lasted until 1969.
The Flight was the joint inspiration of Dr. Soiland, who
had been instrumental in the selection of the Snowbird
as the monotype for the 1932 Olympics, and of Harry
Welch, ever alert for enjoyable ways to advertise Newport
Harbor.

During the 1935-36 dredging the Irvine Company's
Linda Isle was formed. James Irvine Jr., son of James
Irvine II, had been a member of the Orange County Harbor Commission and his father's representative in working out trades and compromises necessary so that "the
harbor could be constructed along sound engineering
lines and the channels be straight and of the proper
width." To provide permanent new roads for Harbor
Island and Beacon Bay, Bayside Drive was moved. A
newly dredged channel created an island from the side
of what had previously been a marshy peninsula. Long
called Shark Island, it was given the name of Linda Isle
in 1949. The Irvine Company bought considerable

dredged material which was placed at Bayshores and on other lowlands. After the death of James Irvine Jr., in 1935, his father devoted more of his own attention to plans for the future development of his Newport Harbor properties.

The completed Newport Harbor with its long jetties, deep channels, anchorages, and newly widened peninsula beach was dedicated on May 23, 1936. When President Roosevelt pressed a telegraph key on his White House desk the Coast Guard cutter *Hermes,* outside Newport Harbor, sounded its cannon to signal the beginning of the most impressive yacht parade Southern California had ever seen. At the lead came the *Memory,* skippered by her owner, George Rogers, honorary captain of the port. The 3600 residents of Newport Beach had little idea of the future ahead for the harbor they had created through years of work and sacrifice. For the moment they thanked George Rogers, having already erected a monument in his honor at the shore end of the west jetty.

When the monument was first proposed, Rogers had suggested that perhaps a plaque might list the names of all those who had lost their lives in the Newport Bay entrance. As soon as he saw that the only name on it was his own, he turned to Richard Patterson and said, "I wish the name on it had been my son's."[8] One afternoon, a few weeks later, Rogers and his daughter went for a cruise on the *Memory.* It was his last voyage. He died, it is said, just as the *Memory* crossed the place in the entrance where his son had been lost ten years earlier.

The Depression Brings a Surprise

NEWPORT HARBOR, the finest yachting and recreational facility on the Pacific Coast, was tested in the years that followed its dedication — first by a hurricane and then by World War II. On September 20, 1939, fierce gales struck Southern California at the end of nine days of sweltering temperatures. Hundreds were on the ocean in small boats. Many who should have remained at sea until the storm passed struggled through mountainous waves in the Newport Harbor entrance which all but hid the jetties from sight. William Bartholomae, one of the area's most colorful yachtsmen, disregarding the advice of his skipper, brought his 140-foot *Paragon* into the entrance where she went aground and sank. The 35-foot *Jolly Tom* struck the west jetty and capsized, throwing seven people into the water. One drowned. John Lugo and Ralph Dawson kept the others afloat on surfboards until help came.

As night fell, many boats were missing from Newport Harbor. No one knew whether their occupants had drowned or were riding out the storm at sea. Among the missing vessels was Joseph A. Beek's *Vamos*, experiencing "the most thrilling adventure of its career."

Flight of the Snowbirds, an annual young people's sailing race held from 1935 until 1969.

At the end of a three-day cruise to Santa Cruz Island, Beek had left his passengers at the Santa Monica pier and started for Newport Harbor with a crew of one. Beek recalled that suddenly, about noon, "the wind began blowing from the southeast with peculiar wisps of white cloud spiraling from the sky. This wind met the *Vamos* just as it was leaving Santa Monica." As the gale grew worse, Beek towed a dismasted sail boat with a young couple aboard into Santa Monica Harbor. After towing a fishing boat ashore, he saw a capsized Delta dinghy. Clinging to the boat was Hugh McLachlan. Climbing aboard the *Vamos*, he said to the skipper, "Gosh! you look good to me!" Beek replied, at the height of the storm, "I'm always being complimented on my good looks."

"Well," shouted McLachlan, "you look like God to me." While the *Vamos* was towing the dinghy to port, the line parted three times. Each time "McLachlan went overboard and in that boiling sea made the lines fast again."[1] Tied to a buoy, the *Vamos* spent the night in Santa Monica Harbor, where heavy rain fell. The sea was quiet the next day when Beek approached Newport Harbor and saw the ravages of the storm. The outer five hundred feet of the old McFadden wharf were gone, and the Balboa pier virtually destroyed. Extensive beach erosion had taken place. Rocks at the ends of both jetties had been

Newport dorymen beached their boats in 1941, "for the duration" of World War II.

The Rendezvous ballroom, Balboa, where "big name" bands played during the 1930s and 1940s.

washed out of place. Inside the harbor Beek saw the "upperstructure of the palatial *Paragon* . . . a grim reminder of the destruction of property and the loss of life which the hurricane had wrought."

In 1940 the jetties were repaired and new piers built at Balboa and Newport. Newport Harbor, home of 1341 pleasure craft and 273 fishing boats, was host to nearly a thousand Sea Scouts at a western states rendezvous. Errol Flynn, James Cagney, Dick Powell, Leo Carrillo, and Jascha Heifetz owned yachts at Newport, while the war in Europe gave rise to rumors that the upper bay would become a naval base. Dr. Albert Soiland, a personal friend of President Roosevelt, was said to be in Washington to interest the government in a west coast Annapolis at Newport Harbor. Newspapers announced the establishment of the Santa Ana Army Air Base in Costa Mesa. At Newport Beach the South Coast Company began building mine sweepers and aircraft rescue boats for the Navy. Wages rose to 65c an hour at the local fish canneries.

On December 7, 1941, the world learned by radio of the Japanese attack on Pearl Harbor. Harbor Master Thomas Bouchey closed Newport Harbor at 12:30 p.m. The U.S. Coast Guard set up headquarters at Collins Castle and at the Gillette house on the peninsula, overlooking the harbor entrance. A few citizens moved away, fearing enemy attacks on the coastline. Newport Beach residents guarded their water supply against possible sabotage, scanned the skies for enemy aircraft, hooded street lights, blacked out the windows of their houses, and swathed automobile headlamps in blue cellophane so that no light could be seen from out at sea. The Coast Guard permitted no boats to enter or leave the harbor until credentials were presented at a barge in the entrance. Newport's dory fishermen, who had gone to sea through the peninsula surf at dawn every morning for more than fifty years, beached their boats and fished from commercial fishing vessels.

Shipyard and cannery workers, families of servicemen stationed nearby, and employees of aircraft and defense industries sought housing in the Newport Harbor area. For the first time in its history, the city found itself without winter residential vacancies. Newport Beach's boat-building industry expanded rapidly, turning out cargo carriers, fishing vessels, and small naval ships of all kinds. The canneries and fishing fleet were given priorities as essential wartime industries. Both flourished as never before. Thousands of soldiers, sailors, and marines danced to "big name" bands at the Rendezvous Ballroom and visited the USO at the corner of Main Street and Balboa Boulevard.

Yachting activities in Southern California came almost to a standstill. Pleasure boats banished from San Pedro and Wilmington "for the duration" sailed down the coast, under escort, to Newport Harbor. None left the harbor unless needed by the armed services. Inside the bay, however, where daytime sailing was permitted, seventy Snowbirds raced in the 1943 Flight of the Snowbirds. Many men and boys who had learned to sail on Newport Harbor gave valiant service on Army, Navy, and Merchant Marine ships during World War II. When it was over they came home to find that once-sleepy Newport Beach had become a flourishing city with a population of 10,000.

On April 1, 1946, "strange, swelling waves pulsated every fifteen minutes" at Newport Beach and elsewhere along the California coastline. Tides were higher than normal. The "seismic sea waves" were a *tsunami*, sometimes mistakenly called a tidal wave. A movement of the sea bottom off the Alaskan coast had given rise to a violent earthquake and to the tsunami, that had caused tremendous loss of life and property in the Hawaiian Islands on April 1. The long, fast tsunami waves did no damage along the California coast, but the phenomenon attracted wide interest.

Newport Harbor

McFaddens' wharf (repaired and remodeled by the city in 1922) lasted until the hurricane of 1939 swept away five hundred feet of its outer end. Today's municipal pier was built the following year.

Sea Nymph's Chariot, Tournament of Lights, 1947. The tournament,
an illuminated boat parade, was an annual event until 1950.

The postwar years were marked in Newport Beach by the passing of several men long identified with the harbor. Among them were John McMillan, once a sailor at Newport Landing, Lew Wallace, early leader of the harbor boosters, and Dr. Albert Soiland, Southern California's respected yachting pioneer. When World War II was over, Soiland, in failing health, left his large estate to establish an institute for cancer research and treatment. Sending a farewell note to fellow yachtsmen saying that he would see them in the fall if all went well, he boarded a freighter bound for his native Norway where he died a few weeks later. Soiland's ashes were returned to California and scattered at sea, between Newport Harbor and Catalina, by some of his old friends from the Newport Harbor Yacht Club.

World War II was a turning point in the history of the Newport Harbor area. Service men and defense workers by the thousands remained in California. In the late 1940s Orange County farmlands began giving way to industries, housing tracts, shopping centers, and freeways. The city of Newport Beach gradually expanded its boundaries from water-oriented areas to the hills and mesa above. The influx of a large and affluent population sent real estate values to heights never dreamed of by early developers. Boat builders and sailmakers moved to inland towns, expanding operations to meet an almost overwhelming demand for pleasure craft of all kinds. For Newport Harbor a new era had begun.

Chronology

1776   Franciscan fathers of San Juan Capistrano Mission begin administration of Newport Bay area.

1810   Spanish land grant of *Rancho Santiago de Santa Ana* (including the Newport mesa and western mainland shoreline of Newport Bay), to José Antonio Yorba and Juan Pablo Peralta.

1842   Mexican land grant of *Rancho San Joaquin* (including the Newport Upper Bay and most of the mainland shoreline of lower bay), to José Andrés Sepúlveda.

1860   First attempt by U.S. Coast Survey to make a preliminary examination of the Santa Ana River estuary (lower bay).

1864   Newport Bay holdings of José Sepúlveda sold to Flint, Bixby, and Irvine. (James Irvine obtains partners' interests in 1876).

1868   Rancho Santiago de Santa Ana partitioned, its holdings bordering Newport Bay going to Flint, Bixby and Irvine, and to attorneys Andrew Glassell and Albert B. Chapman.

1870   The steamer *Vaquero* enters Newport Bay; Newport Landing established on the inner shores. Newport Bay named.

1872   *Vaquero* is sold; little if any activity on Newport Bay for three years.

1875   Newport Landing reopened by James and Robert McFadden. First hydrographic survey of the bay. First arrival of the steamer *Newport*.

1878   Steamer *Newport* sold to Pacific Coast Steamship Company, but continues on San Francisco-Newport run until 1889.

1887   Survey by W. H. H. Benyuard of U.S. Army Corps of Engineers, to determine feasibility of U.S. government-financed improvements to Newport Bay. Estimated cost: $1,200,000. Failing to obtain a federal appropriation for this work, the McFaddens build an ocean wharf in the summer and fall of 1888.

1889   McFadden brothers move their shipping business from inside the bay to new "outside landing" on peninsula ocean front.

1891   Completion of Santa Ana and Newport Railway. Wharf damaged when outer 600 feet washed away by storm on February 22, but repairs soon made.

1892   James McFadden receives title to peninsula from 40th St. to 9th St., purchased for a dollar an acre as government swamp and overflow land. Has town site laid out near the wharf, where lots are leased by the year.

1896 James McFadden buys marsh islands in the bay (later dredged and filled as Balboa, Lido, and Harbor islands).

1899 Santa Ana and Newport Railroad and wharf sold to the Southern Pacific.

1902 Remaining McFadden Newport Bay holdings sold to W. S. Collins and A. C. Hanson.

1903- Establishment of subdivisions of West
1907 Newport, East Newport, Bay Island, Balboa, Corona del Mar, Balboa Island, and Port Orange.

1905 Pacific Electric Railroad reaches Newport.

1906 Pacific Electric rails extended to Balboa. Completion of $15,000 Balboa pavilion.

1912 Newport Harbor lines established. (Ratified by Congress in 1917).

1916 Balboa Island annexed to city of Newport Beach.

1917- Harbor work done by city of Newport
1921 Beach and Orange County includes a 1900-foot-long west jetty, construction of Bitter Point Dam, diversion of Santa Ana River from bay, and dredging of city and county channels. Cost to city, $290,000; to county, $500,000.

1919 City of Newport Beach receives title to tidelands adjacent to its boundaries.

1923 Corona del Mar annexed to city of Newport Beach.

1924 General Lansing Beach, retired chief of the U.S. Army Corps of Engineers, conducts survey and recommends expenditure of $1,200,000 for Newport Harbor improvements.

1926 Defeat of Orange County bond issues to finance $1,200,000 in harbor improvements.

1927 City of Newport Beach votes $500,-000 to extend west jetty and build new east jetty.

1928 Emergency dredging of harbor entrance by Citizens' Harbor Committee.

1929 City of Newport Beach votes $200,000 for entrance dredging and construction of rock groins.

1933 Federal government allocates $1,145,-000, and Orange County voters endorse bond issue of $640,000 to finance final harbor reclamation projects of 1934-36.

1935 Beginning of last big dredging of the lower bay, and extension of jetties.

1936 Dedication of Newport Harbor. Total expenditure on Newport Harbor improvements by private, city, county, and federal agencies between 1906 and 1936: $3,956,800.

Notes

An Uncharted Estuary
PAGES 1 – 2

[1] J. M. Guinn, *Historical and Biographical Record of Southern California* (Chicago: Chapman Publishing Co., 1902), p. 236.

[2] Los Angeles *Star*, September 25, 1870.

[3] United States Coast Survey, *Report of the Superintendent* (Washington: Government Printing Office, 1861), pp. 66-67.

Bolsa de Gengara PAGES 3 – 6

[1] *Decisions of the Department of the Interior and General Land Office in Cases Relating to the Public Lands, From July 1881 to June 1882* (Washington: Government Printing Office, 1887), I, pp. 213-223 Changes in the course of the Santa Ana River following the floods of 1824-25 are also discussed in Guinn, p. 186, col. 2.

[2] H. L. Sherman's theory that the end of the Newport-Balboa peninsula reached only to a point opposite the entrance to the upper bay by 1857 was apparently based upon a literal interpretation (Newport *News*, August 14, 1924) of the rough sketches of the then unsurveyed lower bay that appear on the Hancock plats of Rancho San Joaquin (1858) and Rancho Santiago de Santa Ana (1860). Sherman's beliefs concerning the origin of lower Newport Bay have also been challenged by Newport Beach oceanographer George P. Zebal and others, who base their conclusions upon recent studies of waves and longshore currents affecting the Newport-Balboa peninsula. An interesting and informative discussion of the formation of sandspits, the littoral current, and problems facing Southern California shoreline engineers appears in Willard Bascom's *Waves and Beaches* (New York: Anchor Books, 1964).

[3] Henry R. Wagner, *Juan Rodríquez Cabrillo: Discover of the Coast of California* (San Francisco: California Historical Society, 1941), as quoted in Robert Kirsch and William S. Murphy, *West of the West* (New York: E. P. Dutton, 1967) pp. 26-27.

[4] Los Angeles *Times*, Part II, p. 1, January 23, 1969. The skull of Laguna Woman was discovered by Howard Wilson in 1933 and carbon-dated at the suggestion of L. S. B. Leakey in 1967.

[5] *San Juan Capistrano Mission Records*, Baptism No. 61.

[6] Zephryn Engelhardt, O.F.M., *San Juan Capistrano* (Los Angeles, 1922), pp. 88-91.

[7] Adele Ogden, *The California Sea Otter Trade, 1784-1848* (Berkeley: University of California Press, 1941), pp. 39, 53.

Don José Sepúlveda PAGES 9–14

[1] U.S. National Archives, Private Land Claims, *Rancho San Joaquin*.

[2] Robert Glass Cleland, *The Irvine Ranch* (San Marino: The Huntington Library, 1966), pp. 39-40.

[3] Alfred Robinson, *Life in California* (Oakland, California: Biobooks, 1947), p. 20.

[4] For a description of this house see Don C. Meadows, *The House of Bernardo Yorba* (Santa Ana: Pioneer Press, 1963).

[5] Richard Henry Dana, *Two Years Before the Mast* (Los Angeles: The Ward Ritchie Press, 1964), p. 82.

[6] Alfred Robinson, *Life in California*, p. 25.

[7] U.S. Archives, *Rancho San Joaquin*.

[8] *U.S. Coast Survey*, 1861, pp. 66-67.

[9] John S. Hittell, *The Resources of California* (San Francisco: A. Roman and Company, 1863), p. 9. The correct latitude of Newport Harbor is 33° 36' 20" N.

[10] Guinn, p. 138.

11 Ella A. Ludwig, *History of the Harbor District of Los Angeles* (Los Angeles: Historic Record Co., 1927), p. 333.

12 U.S. Archives, *Rancho San Joaquin*.

Flint, Bixby, and Irvine
PAGES 15 – 17

1 Information from Jim Sleeper, former staff historian of the Irvine Company.

2 Santa Ana *Blade*, September 7, 1915.

3 Los Angeles *Star*, December 19, 1868.

San Joaquin Bay in 1869
PAGES 19 – 20

1 Harvey Rice, *Letters from the Pacific Slope* (New York: D. Appleton & Company, 1870), pp. 95-115.

2 *Ibid.*

3 Unidentified clipping, Santa Ana *Register*.

The Steamer *Vaquero*
PAGES 21 – 23

1 San Diego *Union*, November 7, 1868.

2 Jerry MacMullen, *The Southwest Corner: Historical Sketches Appearing in the Sunday Edition of the San Diego Union*, VII, 1962. Typescript at the Serra Museum, San Diego, Calif.

3 *Alta California*, September 10, 1865.

4 Don W. Stewart, *Frontier Port* (Los Angeles: The Ward Ritchie Press, 1966), p. 115.

5 San Diego *Union*, August 18, 1870.

6 William E. Smythe, *History of San Diego, 1542-1908* (San Diego: The History Company, 1908), p. 369.

7 George Davidson, *Pacific Coast Pilot of California, Oregon, and Washington Territory* (Washington: Government Printing Office, 1869), pp. 16-17.

A New Port PAGES 25 – 27

1 Los Angeles *Star*, September 15, 1870.

2 "James McFadden Gives His Views on the Harbor," Santa Ana *Blade*, September 7, 1915.

3 Los Angeles *Star*, September 28, 1870.

4 Jim Sleeper, *San Joaquin Gazette*, "Newport," 1968.

5 Anaheim *Gazette*, November 26, 1870.

6 Terry Stephenson, "John Cubbon Gives Vivid Picture of Early Days," Santa Ana *Register*, March 13, 1920.

7 Walter Tedford, "The Tedford Family," *Orange County History Series* (Santa Ana: Orange County Historical Society, 1931), I, p. 92.

8 Anaheim *Gazette*, May 20, 1871.

9 *Ibid.*, September 9 and 16, 1871.

10 San Diego *Union*, November 10, 1871.

11 Anaheim *Gazette*, December 14, 1871.

12 *L. E. Smith and L. Halberstadt vs. S. S. Dunnells, Master of the Steamer Vaquero* (Los Angeles District [now Superior] Court, Case #1964, filed April 18, 1872) and *Richard Heimann et. al. vs. S. S. Dunnells* (Case #1967, filed April 18, 1872). Sheriff's Writ of Attachment filed April 18, 1872).

13 San Diego *World*, August 6, 1872.

The McFadden Brothers
PAGES 29 – 33

1 Anaheim *Gazette*, November 16, 1872.

2 Terry E. Stephenson, "Robert McFadden Tells of Early Day Shipping," Santa Ana *Register*, March 27, 1920.

3 "Recollections of Arthur James McFadden," (UCLA, Oral History Program, 1965), pp. 20-21.

4 Anaheim *Gazette*, April 18, 1874.

5 *Ibid.*

6 Information on the steamer *Newport* was supplied by Ivan L. Peterson of Burlingame, Calif.

7 Stephenson-Cubbon Interview, 1920.

8 Stephenson-McFadden Interview, 1920.

9 Santa Ana *Blade*, September 7, 1915.

10 Los Angeles *Star*, May 8, 1875.

11 Stephenson-McFadden Interview, 1920.

12 Anaheim *Gazette*, September 11, 1875.

The Steamer *Newport*
PAGES 35 – 39

[1] Santa Ana *Register*, June 9, 1919.
[2] Guinn, p. 234.
[3] Anaheim *Gazette*, October 7, 1876.
[4] Santa Ana *Blade*, September 7, 1915.
[5] Stephenson-McFadden Interview, 1920.
[6] Anaheim *Gazette*, April 1, 1877.

Tom Rule
PAGES 41 – 45

[1] H. L. Sherman, *History of Newport Beach* (Los Angeles: Times-Mirror Press, 1931), p. 13
[2] Anaheim *Gazette*, March 22, 1879.
[3] Terry E. Stephenson, "Former Resident of this City Tells of Beating of Kearney by Tom Rule," Santa Ana *Register*, Feb. 7, 1920.
[4] George Davidson, *Pacific Coast Pilot* (Washington: Government Printing Office, 1889), pp. 34-35.
[5] Stephenson-McFadden Interview, 1920.

McFaddens' Wharf
PAGES 47 – 55

[1] Journal kept by James McFadden, January-February, 1889.
[2] Arthur J. McFadden, "Reminiscences," p. 53.
[3] Los Angeles *Times*, June 2, 1892.
[4] Jim Sleeper, "The Strange Cruise of the Last Chance," *Orange Countiana* (Orange County Historical Society, 1973), I, p. 5.
[5] Santa Ana *Blade*, September 7, 1915.

A New Century
PAGES 57 – 61

[1] Los Angeles *Times* Midwinter Issue, January 1, 1899, p. 10.
[2] Guinn, pp. 417-418.
[3] Commodore Albert Soiland, *The Saga of Newport Bay and Newport Harbor Yacht Club* (Los Angeles, 1936), pp. 7-10.

Balboa Island
PAGES 63 – 66

[1] Joseph Allan Beek, "My First Day at Balboa," Newport *News*, May 21, 1936.
[2] Sherman, pp. 169-70.
[3] Newport *News*, October 3, 1914.
[4] Joseph Allan Beek, *Balboa Island Yarns* (Newport Beach, 1950). pp. 5-6.
[5] Newport *News*, May 27, 1937.

Duck Hunting, Yachting, and Aviation
PAGES 67 – 73

[1] T. B. Talbert, *My Sixty Years in California* (Huntington Beach, 1952), p. 40.
[2] Newport *News*, July 8, 1911.
[3] Soiland, p. 19.
[4] Newport *News*, June 1, 1912.
[5] Beek, *Balboa Island Yarns*, pp. 14-15.
[6] Newport *News*, May 8, 1912.
[7] *Ibid.*, November 23, 1912.
[8] *Ibid.*, February 8, 1913.
[9] *Ibid.*, July 6, 1914.
[10] *Ibid.*, April 5, 1913.
[11] *Ibid.*, November 6, 1915.

The Floods of 1914-16
PAGES 75 – 80

[1] Talbert, pp. 57, 63.
[2] Arthur J. McFadden, p. 11.
[3] Newport *News*, March 7, 1914.
[4] *Ibid.*, May 22, 1915.
[5] *Ibid.*, June 4, 1915.
[6] *Ibid.*, January 22, 1916.
[7] Beek, *Balboa Island Yarns*, pp. 20-21.
[8] Newport *News*, December 29, 1916.

The First Harbor Work
PAGES 81 – 86

[1] Los Angeles *Times*, December 2, 1917.
[2] Newport *News*, June 18, 1920.
[3] *Ibid.*, April 12, 1921.
[4] *Ibid.*, June 4, 1921.
[5] Samuel A. Meyer, *Fifty Golden Years: A History of the City of Newport Beach*, 1906-1956 (Newport Beach, Calif., 1956) pp. 96-100.
[6] Joseph Allan Beek, "Regattas, Past and Present, of Newport Harbor," Newport *News*, Fourth Annual Harbor Edition, August, 1930.

Motion Picture Boats
PAGES 87 – 90

[1] Newport *News*, August 10, 1917.
[2] *Ibid.*, August 15, 1919.
[3] *Ibid.*, October 17, 1919.
[4] *Ibid.*, June 20, 1924.
[5] Sherman, pp. 141-42.

Crossing the Newport Bar in the 1920s
PAGES 93 – 99

[1] Sherman, p. 103.

[2] Meyer, p. 22.

[3] Newport *News,* June 8, 1924.

[4] *Ibid.*

[5] *Ibid.,* June 13, 1924.

[6] *Ibid.,* September 26, 1924.

[7] *Ibid.,* March 17, 1925.

[8] *Ibid.,* October 13, 1925.

[9] *Ibid.,* June 16, 1925.

[10] Beek, "Regattas Past and Present."

[11] Sherman, p. 106.

The Depression Brings a Surprise
PAGES 103 – 109

[1] Newport *News,* July 5, 1928.

[2] *Ibid.,* December 6, 1928.

[3] Beek, *Balboa Island Yarns,* pp. 45-46.

[4] Balboa Tournament of Lights Association Brochure, 1948.

[5] Newport *News,* January 12, 1933.

[6] *Ibid.*

[7] Los Angeles *Times,* January 11, 1934.

[8] Conversation with Richard L. Patterson, 1966.

Newport Harbor
PAGES 111 – 114

[1] Joseph Allan Beek, "Saga of the *Vamos,*" Unpublished manuscript, 1950.

Photograph Credits

The photographs in this book have been reproduced through the courtesy of the following individuals and institutions: Mrs. Joseph A. Beek, pages 56, 78, 79, 84, 85, 86, 88, 95, 99, 110, 114; Mrs. William Bertuleit, 112 (top); Mr. Rufus B. Courtney, 45; Mr. M. L. De Grasse, 90; Mrs. W. B. Lockett, 53 (lower left); Mrs. C. W. Messing, 68, 83 (top); Mr. George W. Peabody, 60, 77, 94, 96; Miss Edna Phelps, frontispiece and 97; Mr. E. H. Salter, 48, 50; Mr. James D. Sleeper, 53 (upper right), 61; Mr. and Mrs. Howard L. Smith, 18, 46, 48-49 (center), 49; and Mrs. William B. Worden, 28.

Newport Beach Historical Society, 65, 89, 92, 100, 104, 108, 112, 113; Special Collections of the Library at U.C. Irvine, 2, 82, 83 (lower), 105 (Cochems Collection), 52 (Louise Tubbs Collection); Special Collections of the Library at California State University, Fullerton, 51; Charles W. Bowers Memorial Museum, Santa Ana, 10, 11, 44, 52 (top), 53 (upper left), 62; Anaheim Public Library, 59; Bancroft Library, Berkeley, 8, 53 (lower right); The Irvine Company, 16, 55; County of Orange, Harbors, Beaches, and Parks District, 22; California State Library, Sacramento, 52 (lower right), 72; Mariners Museum, Newport News, Va., 34; Los Angeles County Museum of Natural History, 74; Title Insurance and Trust Company of San Diego, 23; Teledyne Geotronics, Long Beach, 102.

Index

TYPE : Palatino phototype
PAPER : Warrens Olde Style
DESIGN : Dana C. Cordrey/Sultana Press
MANUFACTURED BY : Premier Printing Corporation/Sultana Press